"Fr. Paul Turner's latest exploration of the revised liturgical books skillfully weaves the history of welcoming the already baptized into the Catholic church with the how and why of the rite today. With his characteristically well-researched explanations of what has changed, what hasn't, and the theological and pastoral reasonings for both, Fr. Turner not only breaks open the liturgical text, but offers pragmatic advice for preparing candidates, celebrating their reception, and helping them live out their communion fully."

— Rev. Michael L. Lewis, pastor, Most Holy Trinity Catholic Church, and director of the Office of Worship for the Diocese of El Paso, Texas

"In *Full Communion with Us*, Fr. Paul Turner brings much-needed clarity to the often-confused practice of celebrating sacraments with baptized candidates. He carefully distinguishes their path from that of catechumens, honoring their prior Christian journey of faith while faithfully explaining the Church's vision for their reception into full communion. Fr. Turner's clear, pastoral style makes this book a must-read for every parish serious about welcoming baptized Christians into the full communion of the Catholic Church with the dignity, understanding, and care they deserve."

— Nick Wagner, codirector of Team Initiation and author of *Field Hospital Catechesis: The Core Content for RCIA Formation*

Full Communion with Us

The Reception of Candidates in the OCIA

Paul Turner

LITURGICAL PRESS
Collegeville, Minnesota

litpress.org

Cover art courtesy of Getty Images.

Library of Congress Cataloging-in-Publication Data

Names: Turner, Paul, 1953– author
Title: Full communion with us : the reception of candidates in the OCIA / Paul Turner.
Description: Collegeville, Minnesota : Liturgical Press, [2025] | Summary: "In Full Communion with Us, Paul Turner provides an in-depth analysis of the pages of the Order of Christian Initiation of Adults that concern baptized candidates, with guidance that takes seriously both the liturgical rites and the Catholic Church's ecumenical commitments. Those who are preparing the formation as well as the liturgical celebrations pertaining to baptized candidates will find this an invaluable resource"— Provided by publisher.
Identifiers: LCCN 2025014126 (print) | LCCN 2025014127 (ebook) | ISBN 9798400801662 trade paperback | ISBN 9798400801679 epub
Subjects: LCSH: Catholic Church. Ordo initiationis Christianae adultorum | Catholic Church—Membership | Initiation rites—Religious aspects—Catholic Church | BISAC: RELIGION / Christian Rituals & Practice / General | RELIGION / Christianity / Catholic
Classification: LCC BX2045.I553 T87 2025 (print) | LCC BX2045.I553 (ebook) | DDC 268/.82—dc23/eng/20250613
LC record available at https://lccn.loc.gov/2025014126
LC ebook record available at https://lccn.loc.gov/2025014127

IN MEMORIAM

ELISABETHÆ HEIDLERÆ

QVÆ VISIONEM MVNDI PERFECTIORIS VIDIT

FIDEM SVAM VIXIT

FAMILIAM SVAM AMAVIT

PEREGRINVM EXCEPIT

ALIOS CHRISTVM SEQVI ADIVVIT

ET HVNC AVCTOREM

PER SEMITAS PVLCHRAS INTELLIGENDI
SPIRITVM HVMANVM DVXIT

CLARIFICANDÆ EI MINISTERII PASTORALIS FINES

Contents

Abbreviations

DAPNE	Directory for the Application of Principles and Norms on Ecumenism (Washington, DC: United States Conference of Catholic Bishops, 1993)
GIRM	The General Instruction of the Roman Missal
LM	*Lectionary for Mass*
OCIA	*The Order of Christian Initiation of Adults* (Collegeville, MN: Liturgical Press, 2024)
OConf	*The Order of Confirmation* (Washington, DC: United States Conference of Catholic Bishops, 2016)
RCIA	*Rite of Christian Initiation of Adults* (Collegeville, MN: Liturgical Press, 1988)
RM	Roman Missal

Introduction

"Do you have a church?"

I keep that question handy when I meet someone. I have it ready when I get to know a new neighbor, make a chance encounter at a party, or fall into conversation with a stranger standing in some line. Especially if they've asked about my work, I'll tell them I'm a Catholic priest, and then I may ask, "Do you have a church?"

People usually receive that question respectfully. It touches something in them that they may or may not have articulated before. Sometimes it opens a fresh willingness to share. I may hear things like, "Well, I used to go more often." Or, "My family and I belong to a synagogue."

If they have a faith community, I respond favorably. I don't twist arms. I open doors. "Well, you're welcome at our church if you ever want to visit."

On some rare occasions, the person may say rather defiantly, "Well, I'm not a Catholic." If they say that, I may smile and respond, "I can take care of that." It breaks the ice.

This book concerns helping Christians of other denominations who have an interest in reception into the Catholic Church. The process involves both catechetical formation and ritual celebration. Before those of us in pastoral ministry can offer catechesis about Catholicism or share the sacraments with new members, we need to offer an invitation. Many of us Catholics are shy to do that, even among other Christians.

The Catholic Church revised its various rites for adult initiation in the 1970s. Since then, many books, articles, conferences, and ministers in parishes have spotlighted the formation of inquirers who are unbaptized: the catechumens.

Indeed, a large part of our ritual book, *The Order of Christian Initiation of Adults* (OCIA), describes how to move catechumens through the various stages of formation toward initiation. Their ultimate baptism dramatically crowns their yearning for Christ. Theirs is truly a path of conversion—from life outside the sacraments toward membership in the Body of Christ, from principles oriented around other goals toward those fulfilling the gospel, from susceptibility to sin toward gratitude for grace.

Some others interested in Catholicism have already been baptized in another Christian denomination. The OCIA calls this group "candidates." They follow a similar path, but their goal is different. Already members of the Body of Christ, they are seeking to join its specific expression in the Catholic Church. Because the unbaptized and the baptized ultimately seek the same membership and communion, many parishes combine the formation and celebrations for both groups.

Adult baptism normally takes place during the Easter Vigil. Both the OCIA and the Roman Missal (RM) call for it that way. St. Paul told the Romans that, through baptism, those united with Christ in a death like his also share in a resurrection like his (Rom 6:5, 4, cited in OCIA, Christian Initiation: General Introduction, 6). Easter provides the perfect frame for this sacrament.

Many Catholic parishes of the United States therefore follow a school-year model of formation for Christian initiation. They begin sessions in the fall, and they wrap up after Easter in the spring. If new inquirers present themselves after these scheduled sessions have begun, parish leaders may keep them occupied in some way but often defer their participation in a formation group until the following fall. This especially inconveniences baptized candidates, who already enjoy life in Christ, and whose reception is not bound to Easter.

In many Catholic parishes, catechumens and candidates form a single group, following the same school-year model and receiving the same formation, regardless of the experience that each may bring. If they are short on staff or volunteers, parishes may not have the personnel to offer separate tracks for individuals or groups seeking membership. Besides, both catechumens and candidates need a grounding in what it is to be Catholic, so leaders often engage them in elements of formation together. Members of this combined catechetical group frequently form a strong bond among themselves as they explore the individual yearnings of the spiritual life and satisfy their desire to belong. They grow in personal faith and ecclesial experience.

However, there are significant differences between catechumens and candidates. Candidates already have a valid baptism. They share in the life of grace made open to them in the resurrection of Christ. The climax of their formation comes in their reception into the full communion of the Catholic Church, followed by the sacraments of confirmation and Holy Communion. That ceremony is not connected to Easter as is adult baptism. Candidates may be entitled to a more specific process of formation and more varied opportunities for reception into the full communion of the Catholic Church.

This book will review the parts of the OCIA devoted to candidates. It will help you think more precisely about their formation. It may open previously unnoticed doors to the celebration of their reception. It will guide the pastoral care you give those who seek the full communion of the church and sacramental communion in the Body and Blood of Christ.

Nonetheless, candidates will not take advantage of any of this unless they feel invited. Some parishes rest on a passive approach to evangelization. Ministers wait in the office until an interested person sends an email, places a phone call, or shows up at the front door. Once visitors tell such ministers that they'd like more information, the process begins.

However, true evangelization requires a more active outreach. A well-prepared parish website may guide those seeking more information about the Catholic Church and how people live their faith in your parish. Some inquirers will review your website to find an easy way to begin. They would benefit from a warm online invitation with a clear description of the process in your parish. The weekly bulletin may also carry contact information. A brief announcement at Mass may alert people that those interested in joining the church are meeting this week. All of these are ways that the parish community may clear a path for those who are already seeking a way inside.

Still, nothing replaces a direct invitation. This may flow from ordinary conversation. "How does your faith influence your decisions?" "Do your kids have questions relating to faith?" "Would you like to come to church with me next Sunday?" When Catholics are comfortable talking about their faith, they'll find others ready to engage.

Formation for the sacraments and initiation into the sacraments begins with an invitation. In one sense, the summons is already there. Christ has opened the door, but he uses the voices and hands of his disciples to show the way inside. He has touched the hearts of all with a special longing for something more. He needs us to invite others—even other Christians—to hear more of the good news of his life, message, and resurrection.

1

The Basics

The OCIA

Among its liturgical reforms, the Second Vatican Council's Constitution on the Sacred Liturgy authorized a restoration of a multi-staged process for the initiation of adult Christians, marked by sacred rites at specific intervals of time (64). In its earliest centuries, Christianity had crafted such an approach, which then fell into disuse by the Middle Ages—primarily because the successful spread of the gospel had shifted the age of typical prospects for baptism from adulthood to infancy. However, the church's historical trove of liturgical texts from that early period has enriched today's process of conversion with a series of rites based on the past, renewed for the present, and adaptable for individual circumstances.

As with all official books for worship in the Catholic Church, the Vatican first issued its revised order for initiation in Latin in what it calls a typical edition. This was published in the year 1972. The release came on January 6, the traditional solemnity of the Epiphany of the Lord, commemorating the day when the infant Christ was first revealed to previously unbelieving nations represented by the visiting magi. Christ still reveals himself to people who seek him through a journey made in faith.

The bishops of the United States published a provisional English translation in 1974, which caught the attention of leaders in many parishes who started implementing it right away. In 1988 a new English translation, now official, appeared in a much-enhanced edition. This publication distributed parts of the typical edition's introduction across pertinent sections of the book—keeping all of the material, but arranging it differently.

The 1988 translation also included material proper to the United States not found in the typical edition. It added preliminary rites for candidates who had already been baptized in other Christian denominations, but who had received little subsequent formation in the faith. These were adapted from the preliminary rites for catechumens. These adapted rites responded to a pastoral situation in the United States—the large number of other Christians wishing to become Catholic. Those preparing the translation apparently judged that the order of service for receiving these Christians, a single ritual tucked into the appendix of the typical edition, could be favorably enhanced with additional rites that the revisers never considered.

The 1988 book also created extensive commentary on these new rites to guide ministers using the material. It even showed how to combine those adapted preliminary rites for candidates with the original ones for unbaptized Christians, in order to assist communities advancing both groups at the same time. These adapted and combined rites in the specific English translation for the United States fostered the pastoral practice of keeping all catechumens and candidates in the same formational group.

The same translation also included combined rites at the Easter Vigil, inserting the reception of previously baptized Christians into that service for the first time in Christian history. Even the third edition of the Roman Missal, which makes generous room for the initiation rites of those completing the catechumenate, gives no instructions for the reception of candidates. That is only found among the adaptations to the rites of adult initiation that the Vatican approved for usage in the United States.

The 1988 translation was called the *Rite of Christian Initiation of Adults*. People commonly abbreviated it as RCIA. It is a ritual book, sharing the same shelf with titles such as *The Order of Baptism of Children*, *The Order of Confirmation*, and *The Order of Celebrating Matrimony*.

The acronym RCIA should have referred uniquely to the book, as would the acronyms OBC, OConf, and OCM in the above examples. However, "RCIA" came to serve as shorthand for the entire process of initiation: evangelization, catechesis, and ritual stages. Many parishes promoted "RCIA groups" or "RCIA classes," which welcomed those seeking to join the Catholic Church.

Applying the acronym of the book to its attendant catechesis did not happen with other rituals. For example, no one calls marriage preparation OCM. The broader usage of the term RCIA demonstrated the unfamiliarity many people had with the liturgical book and the process it had introduced.

Because of the broad application of the acronym, some people criticized the RCIA for not including more detailed plans of catechesis. However, the RCIA was a ritual book, not a catechetical book. No one expects *The Order of Celebrating Matrimony* to provide a detailed plan for marriage preparation. It gives guidance for catechesis, but it is fundamentally a ritual book.

In Latin, the name of the book that generated the acronym is *Ordo initiationis Christianae adultorum*. Around the year 2000, the Catholic Church revised its rules for translating liturgical texts, calling for a more literal translation of the originals than the first English translations, though fundamentally faithful, had offered. This meant that a book such as *The Rite of Baptism for Children* eventually received a thoroughly new translation under a revised title, *The Order of Baptism of Children*. Similarly,

The Rite of Penance, which guides priests and faithful through the sacrament of reconciliation, became *The Order of Penance.*

The first translators of these books probably thought that "Rite" was more expressive in English than "Order." However, the word "Rite" is also used for classes of churches, such as the Roman Rite and the Byzantine Rite. Besides, within the liturgical books, a "Rite" can refer to a particular ceremony. An "Order," therefore, often signifies a collection of "Rites."

This prompted a change to the title of the RCIA in a revised translation issued in 2024. Now known as *The Order of Christian Initiation of Adults,* the book and the formation it guides immediately became known as the OCIA. Its contents are virtually the same, adding the ceremonies for baptized but uncatechized candidates, as well as distributing the introductory material in the same remixed order.

That order is evident from the double numbering system found in both these editions. The primary numbers on the left side of the page are sequential and are the ones that this book will use for reference. The smaller numbers on the right side of each page identify the corresponding number from the typical edition. The letters "USA" in the right column flag material composed in English by the United States and for the United States. Numbers in the right column preceded by the letter *R* indicate material from the appendix of the typical edition, the original source of the Order of Reception into the Full Communion of the Catholic Church.

The 1988 book concluded with a set of national statutes pertaining to Christian initiation, passed by the bishops of the United States in 1986. Some of these duplicated materials already found in the typical edition. The bishops have therefore reduced the scope of the statutes, clarified some of their points, and repositioned them at the front of the 2024 book as part of the prefatory matter.

The main contribution of the revised book is in the translation, where the style adheres more closely to that of other recent revisions, such as the rituals for baptism, confirmation, and penance. The 2024 book also coordinates more directly with parts of the Roman Missal: its Ritual Masses "For the Conferral of the Sacraments of Christian Initiation," as well as its expanded rubrics for the Easter Vigil. These elaborate the role of deacons, for example, and offer instructions for incorporating newborn infants among those to be baptized.

For the reception of baptized Christians, the 2024 edition retains and refines the reordering found in the 1988 edition. However, it is important to understand the typical edition and its history. After the Second Vatican Council, the development of the revised order of initiation for adults happened at the same time but apart from the development of the revised order for the reception of baptized Christians into the full communion of the Catholic Church. Both were ready in 1972, and the ritual for baptized candidates was added to the ritual for catechumens as an appendix, probably for the sake of convenience.

This typical edition made a sharp distinction between baptized Christians wishing to become Catholic and unbaptized persons preparing for the rites of initiation. Validly baptized Christians already shared membership in the Body of Christ through the first of the initiation sacraments. Their case formed an appendix to the concerns that more fittingly belong under the category of the Christian initiation of unbaptized adults.

The decision to treat baptized Christians differently but respectfully fit clearly within the view of the ecumenical movement, which gained strength at the same time as the liturgical movement. The very division of rites within the outline of the book indicated that those who shared a common baptism would not be considered equivalent to the unbaptized.

Now, however, due to the reordering of content in the English translations of the United States, the OCIA refers rather evenly to both groups—the unbaptized and the baptized. Those using the book therefore owe special attention to the baptized candidates out of respect for their status, the advances in ecumenism, and the preservation of the original vision that the typical edition strove to enshrine.

Terminological Distinctions

"Candidates"

Several terms distinguish the baptized from the unbaptized inquirers. Most foundationally, the unbaptized are called "catechumens" throughout most of their formation, and the baptized are called "candidates."

The 1988 English translation caused some confusion because the typical edition in Latin applied the word "candidates" also to unbaptized persons who were not yet catechumens. There were candidates for the catechumenate and candidates for reception.

The same word appears in other ritual books, where "candidates" refers to those preparing for confirmation and for ordination, for example. It simply means a person in formation toward a particular ritual step. The Latin original applied the same word to validly baptized Christians from other denominations for the same reason: they were in formation for reception. It meant nothing more than that.

However, because in the United States the word "candidate" was being used as a counterpoint to "catechumen" to distinguish the baptized from the unbaptized among those seeking membership in the Catholic Church, the revised translation has accordingly restricted the use of the term. Where the previous translation used "candidates" for those not yet baptized, the 2024 translation uses "inquirers" or "catechumens." The word "candidate" now has a more specific meaning within Christian initiation than the typical edition imagined, but the revision helps those in the field to distinguish the two groups.

"Evangelization"

"Evangelization" is a term for a period that the OCIA assigns only to the unbaptized. At the beginning of their formation, they come as inquirers (39) and begin the stage of the precatechumenate. At that time, evangelization happens, "in which the living God is confidently and constantly proclaimed, together with the one whom he sent for the salvation of all, Jesus Christ, so that, as the Holy Spirit opens their hearts, non-Christians may be freely converted to the Lord" (36).

This paragraph cites the Second Vatican Council's Decree on the Missionary Activity of the Church, *Ad Gentes*, number 13. It shows that some inquirers have virtually no conscious foundation in faith. Christianity offers them a trinitarian framework to shape their outlook on the world.

Catechists may therefore guide inquirers through this period of evangelization by inviting them to ask themselves the most basic questions about faith:

- Who is God?
- Is the creator of the universe still active in the world?
- Does this God care for me?
- Who was Jesus?
- What does it mean to say that he was the Son of God?
- Is the testimony of his resurrection reliable?
- How does his resurrection apply to me?
- Do I really have hope of eternal life?

The Holy Spirit may guide responses to these questions through the assistance of catechists and sponsors. Such parish ministers should not presume that inquirers already have a grasp on these basic matters. Guiding them through fundamental spiritual reflection is how OCIA 39 sees evangelization.

However, in popular usage, the word "evangelization" sometimes describes an outreach to those who are already baptized, but whose practice of the faith has become tepid. That is more precisely a "re-evangelization" of those who have already heard the message of the gospel, though it did not completely take root even after their baptism.

The OCIA sees evangelization as more foundational. Etymologically, it suggests bringing the gospel to places where its light had not yet reached—the first dictionary definition upon which future metaphors are based.

Throughout, the OCIA presumes that those who are unbaptized have not yet heard about Christ, and that their early formation focuses on coming to know the gospel. In practice, that is not always the case. Many of those who call themselves Christians have never presented themselves for baptism. They heard the gospel through their family and friends, perhaps even at church. They have shaped their lives according to the teaching of Christ. They just never got baptized. For them, evangelization happened a long time ago. But the OCIA still engages them in a fundamental conversation to ensure that they possess the foundations of faith in the Holy Trinity.

Baptized candidates by definition are already beyond the stage of evangelization. However, many of them may benefit from reflecting on the same questions.

"Order of Reception"

When a person from another Christian denomination becomes Catholic, the ceremony is called the Order of Reception into the Full Communion of the Catholic Church of Those Already Validly Baptized. However, for the Spanish edition in the United States, which also received a new translation in 2024, the title is *Rito de recepción a la plena comunión con la Iglesia católica de los cristianos bautizados.*

Immediately, one can see that the Spanish translation uses the equivalent of the word "Rite," where the English translation now calls this ceremony an "Order." The 1988 English translation used neither of these words, simplifying the title to Reception of Baptized Christians into the Full Communion of the Catholic Church.

As mentioned above, the word "order" can refer to a collection of rites. In this case, it seems at first that the Spanish translation more correctly includes the reception of a validly baptized Christian among the "rites" within the "order" of Christian initiation.

However, the typical edition in Latin uses the word for "order" in the title of this particular ceremony. This reflects how, after the Second Vatican Council, the revisers developed this liturgy apart from *The Order of Christian Initiation of Adults*. The reception of those validly baptized called for its own order of service, as did the initiation of unbaptized adults.

As revised English translations are now to be more faithful to the Latin original, the 2024 edition has taken the more literal term into the heading, which also helps establish the position of this ceremony as a separate "order," not one of a series of "rites." The appearance of the word *Rito* in the Spanish translation for the United States is therefore probably an oversight. As the revised translation changed the title of the entire book from *Rito* to *Ritual*, signifying a collection of rites, so this liturgy of reception should probably have been called *Ritual*.

A glance at the table of contents of the OCIA shows that the word "order" appears multiple times in the chapter heads. There is an "Order of the Catechumenate Arranged in Steps," which includes several "Rites": Entrance into the Catechumenate, Election or Enrollment of Names, and those of Immediate Preparation. The Order of Initiation for children similarly has internal rites. There are orders of adult initiation that abbreviate or collapse the rites into a single order of service.

The same table of contents assigns the Order of Reception to chapter VI, but in the typical edition it was the appendix. There it more clearly stood out as a separate order of service, quite distinct from the others. Use of the word "order" in the title, then, shows its equivalence to the Order of Initiation.

The previous translation used "order" in another way. It called the first of the rites "Acceptance into the Order of Catechumens." This is now translated as "Entrance into the

Catechumenate" because the word "order" does not appear here in the Latin. In the past, the group of catechumens was considered one among various ranks within the church, thus occupying an order, such as the order of deacons, of priests, or of bishops. OCIA 7a and 7b still use "order of catechumens" this way. However, the rest of the ritual book never uses this expression.

"Communion Of"

Comparing the English and Spanish titles for the Order of Reception reveals another difference. Less obvious than *Rito* is the usage of *con*, which means "with." The English translation more accurately uses the word "of." The baptized Christian is not entering communion "with the Catholic Church," but is being received into the full communion "of the Catholic Church." The Catholic Church does not offer communion "with" other individuals; it receives them into its full communion, within which they may now receive Holy Communion. In English popular usage, some people casually refer to this ceremony as "Full Communion with the Catholic Church," but that is neither its title nor its meaning.

That little preposition packs considerable meaning. Its choice is based on the Second Vatican Council's Dogmatic Constitution on the Church, *Lumen Gentium*, which states that the church subsists in the Catholic Church (8). The council also stated in its Decree on Ecumenism, *Unitatis Redintegratio*, that Christians baptized in other denominations are in communion with the Catholic Church, but this communion is imperfect (3). Thus, a validly baptized candidate already has some communion "with" the Catholic Church but is applying for reception into the full communion "of" the Catholic Church.

The Spanish word for "with" appears in the title of this ceremony inside the ritual book for adult initiation used by other conferences of bishops, notably the one in Spain. The translation for the United States therefore probably copied what others had done, though the meaning is imprecise.

"Already Validly"

In Spanish, then, the complete title translates as *The Rite of Reception of Baptized Christians into the Full Communion with the Catholic Church*. The words for "already validly" are omitted, probably under the influence of the 1988 English translation, which had omitted them as well.

Both of those translations may represent a judgment that two words could be omitted because they are implied. If one has been baptized, one is "already" baptized. If the baptism was not valid, then the person has not been baptized. The revised English translation fittingly reminds the reader that not everyone who underwent a ceremony that someone called baptism has truly been baptized. As will be shown below, an investigation on the validity of the baptism of presumed candidates is timely.

"Converts"

The revised national statutes in the United States repeat a much-overlooked point that has been part of the same body of norms since 1986: "The term 'convert' is reserved strictly for those converted to Christian belief and never used of those baptized Christians who are received into the full communion of the Catholic Church" (norm 18).

In practice, even many who have been received from other denominations erroneously call themselves "converts" to Catholicism. This norm highlights the distinction between those who are already baptized and those undergoing the complete change that baptism alone effects. Baptism *converts* someone from life without Christ to life with Christ. Those who are already Christians do not *convert* to Christ when they became

Catholic. They are received into the full communion of the church.

Problematically, the norm that makes this important declaration does not offer a substitute word. If these new Catholics are not converts, what are they? Neither the norm nor popular conversation offers an alternative.

In a similar way, some of the newly received have mistakenly said that they were "confirmed" Catholic, as if the sacrament of confirmation confers membership in the church. It does not. People are first received into the Catholic Church, and then, as Catholics, they receive confirmation.

Most accurately, instead of calling themselves converts, people may say that they were received into the Catholic Church. Who received them? According to OCIA 492, it was the Lord. Certainly, people come of their own free will, as OCIA 490 makes clear, but in the end, the act of reception comes from the Lord.

People in this category have other expressions they may use. Instead of saying, "I'm a convert," they may rightly say, "I was received into the Catholic Church." Or, "I became Catholic."

Baptized Catholics among the Candidates

The Vision of the Typical Edition

The typical edition of the OCIA devotes one chapter to deal with those who were baptized Catholic as infants, but who then received no further catechesis, nor the sacraments of confirmation and Communion. This pastoral circumstance had spread throughout many countries of the world, notably but not exclusively in Latin America. The prevalence of this pastoral situation in the 1960s inside European countries such as Italy, Germany, and France probably led to the development of this chapter. Nothing like it existed before 1972, even though the pastoral situation did.

Throughout the world, many good Catholic parents follow through on their responsibility to have their children baptized. Others may present children for baptism out of pressure from their own parents or from the perceived expectations in society. Some of these parents do not then responsibly provide religious formation for their children. As those children grow older, some of them undergo a spiritual awakening, seek the sacraments they never received—confirmation and the Eucharist—and present themselves for formation.

To be considered candidates for the OCIA, people in this category have to meet several criteria: They were baptized Catholic as a child. They participated in no sacramental formation. They received neither confirmation nor First Communion.

Those who prepared the typical edition must have experienced more pressing concerns about uncatechized Catholics than about additional rites for other Christians. The year after the publication of the typical edition, the Congregation for Divine Worship offered further advice for adapting rites for uncatechized Catholics, as can be seen in the appendix of this book. Because of the attention that the OCIA in the United States gives to candidates validly baptized in other denominations, the pastoral care owed the Catholics for whom the section was originally conceived may be overlooked.

As OCIA 400 notes, the typical edition included yet another group in this category: those who were baptized in danger of death or at the point of death, but who then recovered. This section addresses the pastoral care of these Catholics as well because they may have been baptized without sufficient catechesis. Obviously, this applies to adults in danger of death, not to infants.

A priest who makes the decision to baptize a person in danger of death also has the faculty to confirm (c. 883-3). Canons 889 §2 and 891 remove the usual requirements for catechetical formation and even the minimum age for confirmation in this circumstance. The priest therefore has the faculty to confirm even when baptizing an infant in danger of death. In practice, a priest rarely confirms an infant he baptizes—perhaps because he is unaware of the faculty or because he does not regularly carry chrism as he does the oil of the sick. If the infant recovers, the parents bring the child to the church to celebrate other elements of the order of baptism.

Ordinarily, responsible parents provide catechetical formation for a sick child restored to health, including preparation for confirmation and Communion. This chapter of the OCIA only pertains to children who grew up without those spiritual benefits after their baptism, whether or not it took place in danger of death.

Thus, the typical edition of the OCIA created a special chapter for these Catholics, who, for whatever reason, have a valid baptism but remained uncatechized. Surprising to many who exercise pastoral ministry in the United States, the typical edition of the OCIA never calls these Catholics "candidates."

The Vision in the United States

In the United States, the 1988 English translation of numbers 400–410 made a significant departure from the typical edition. It added validly baptized candidates of other Christian denominations into this chapter. It declared that this section concerned adults baptized as infants "either as Roman Catholics or as members of another Christian community" (RCIA 400).

These few words, unique to the English translation in the United States, grouped all validly baptized but uncatechized Christians into the typical edition's vision of the pastoral concern for uncatechized Catholics. In practice, many of those preparing other Christians for reception assumed that these paragraphs pertained to them all, both the catechized and the uncatechized, and not just to uncatechized Catholics baptized as infants or in danger of death.

As it happens, this decision was not far from the thinking of the Second Vatican Council. When the Constitution on the Sacred Liturgy called for a revision of the various sacramental rites, it grouped baptized infants who survived the threat of death with baptized Christians of other denominations seeking to join the Catholic Church. The same paragraph of the constitution called for new rites for each of these groups (69). Thus even the council bracketed other validly baptized Christians with Catholics baptized in an emergency. Both situations called for appropriate pastoral care and liturgical rites.

Clarifications in the Revised Translation of Chapter V

The first sentence of OCIA 400 now more correctly distinguishes baptized, uncatechized Catholics from baptized, uncatechized Christians of other denominations. The 1988 edition stated that both groups had not received the sacraments of confirmation and Communion as a result of their lack of catechesis. However, the candidates from other denominations do not fit that description. Their non-reception of Catholic confirmation and Communion is a consequence of their membership in another denomination, not of insufficient catechesis. As OCIA 400 now states, those Catholics who did not receive catechesis after baptism "therefore" have not received these other sacraments.

OCIA 400 permits taking the pastoral advice it gives for uncatechized Catholics and applying it to adults baptized in other Christian communities. It may also be used to guide the formation of those baptized in danger of death who subsequently recover, referencing OCIA 374.

OCIA 401 demands "a lengthy period" of formation for uncatechized Catholic adults. It does not make the same requirement for all validly baptized Christians of other denominations. Nor does it require a lengthy period for those who were baptized in danger of or at the point of death. As noted above, the priest who administers baptism in danger of death may also administer confirmation. If the person recovers, catechesis resumes.

Uncatechized Catholic adults are the group that OCIA 402 means when it recommends that the plan for their catechesis correspond "for the most part" to the one established for catechumens. Their baptized status makes them different, but their need for formation is similar.

The same corresponding formation does not apply to those baptized in other denominations who have followed Christ all their lives. The title of this chapter bears witness to this distinction: chapter V concerns uncatechized adults baptized as infants. Many candidates from other Christian denominations already received considerable catechesis. Their formation happens by analogy to those whom chapter V governs, not with an identical design.

While the uncatechized Catholics are in formation for the sacraments, the rest of the community offers them charity and prayer, and ultimately testifies to their readiness (OCIA 403). These practical, spiritual, and catechetical supports, designed for uncatechized, baptized adult Catholics, may apply to uncatechized, baptized candidates of other denominations as well.

When OCIA 404 speaks of the need for a sponsor, this too applies easily to any baptized candidate. OCIA 10 distinguishes sponsors and godparents for the unbaptized: a sponsor may accompany the catechumen for the longer part of the spiritual journey, but a godparent may replace the sponsor for the final stages. All candidates preparing to receive the sacraments of confirmation and Communion may therefore enjoy the support of a sponsor.

It is surprising, then, to see the word "godparent" in OCIA 404 for the one who accompanies an uncatechized, baptized Catholic. This probably relates to the suggestion that the person's baptismal godparent serve again for confirmation, as recommended in *The Order of Confirmation* (5). This, of course, only pertains to the adult Catholic. Not all Christians of other denominations have a baptismal godparent. Even if they did, the new role has to be fulfilled by a Catholic who has received the three sacraments of initiation (c. 874 §1). The one who accompanies a baptized candidate, therefore, is usually a Catholic sponsor.

The Optional Preliminary Rites

As part of their formation for the sacraments, uncatechized Catholic adults are to participate "in certain liturgical rites" (OCIA 401). The typical edition called for these, but gave scant description for them. A fuller description can be found in the appendix of this book. OCIA 405 suggests only that the first of them be "a rite by which adults are received into the community and acknowledge that they have a share in it because they have already been signed with Baptism." Even so, the typical edition did not provide such a rite.

To that end, the 1988 edition for the United States created a suite of rites for such adults—uncatechized Catholics completing the initiation sacraments, and uncatechized Christians of other denominations preparing to be received into the full communion of the Catholic Church (411). These remain in the 2024 edition under new titles, now lettered A, B, C, and D: Rite of Welcoming the Candidates, Rite of Sending the Candidates for the Calling to Continuing Conversion, Rite of Calling the Candidates to Continuing Conversion, and Penitential Rite (Scrutiny). The first of these fulfills the idea that OCIA 405 had submitted.

The typical edition of OCIA 407 permits uncatechized, adult Catholics to participate in the Rites of Handing On, ceremonies that more specifically apply to the catechumens. In the United States, this paragraph also permits candidates to celebrate the remaining adapted rites, depending on their "individual needs and circumstances."

The OCIA in the United States uses the word "candidates" for those who celebrate these adapted rites. The word refers both to the uncatechized Catholic and to the Christian from another denomination. In the typical edition, chapter V pertained only to uncatechized Catholics, which explains why the remainder of this chapter never refers to them as "candidates." In the United States, though, the word covers both groups.

Even though the typical edition detailed no preliminary rites, the Vatican's Dicastery for Divine Worship and the Discipline of the Sacraments has approved all four of them again for use in the United States. These are commonly called "adapted" rites because they draw inspiration from parallel rites designed for the unbaptized.

These four liturgies appear under the heading "Optional Rites for Baptized but Uncatechized Adults." In practice, this designation has often been overlooked. All its points are important: they are for baptized adults who did not receive further catechesis, and they are optional.

These rites are not intended for validly baptized adults of other denominations who have been practicing their faith. However, many parish leaders in the United States have imprecisely used the four of them for all candidates. In defense of the practice, many candidates have testified to the spiritual growth they've received through celebrating these rites, but they have not experienced the alternative, original vision for their ritual journey: an astonishingly grace-filled direct path to the Order of Reception, unencumbered by preliminary rites.

In addition, baptized, uncatechized Catholic adults are to participate in the Liturgy of the Word when the faithful have gathered, such as at Sunday Mass, and in celebrations "designed in a similar way for catechumens" (OCIA 406, citing 81–84). Those celebrations presume that the unbaptized may not yet be ready to pray within the Christian assembly and must learn the basics of prayer (silence, listening, postures, and responses to the dialogues, for example).

OCIA 406 envisions that uncatechized Catholics may need similar training, but it does not make the same assumption for every validly baptized Christian. Hence, in communities where the catechumens gather for celebrations of the Word of God, uncatechized adult Catholics could join them if their circumstances favored it. However, the OCIA recommends dismissing catechumens after the Liturgy of the Word at Sunday Mass (83b), but it never calls for dismissing baptized Christians, especially those who were catechized in areas such as Scripture, worship, and morals in their own denominations.

The Time of Year

The climax of formation "will normally be the Easter Vigil" (OCIA 409). This declaration pertains to baptized, uncatechized adult *Catholics*, not to the candidates of other denominations. OCIA 408 similarly promotes inserting the formation of these Catholics into the liturgical year, when their final preparation in Lent prepares them for the sacrament of penance. As OCIA 409 notes, when a bishop is not present at the Easter Vigil, the priest needs to receive from him the faculty to confirm any previously baptized Catholic.

The revised translation of OCIA 408 and 409 more clearly shows that this chapter never promoted the reception of validly baptized Christians at the Easter Vigil. As noted above, even the third edition of the Roman Missal, which enhanced the rubrics for the Easter Vigil by expanding the role of the deacon and clarifying the procedures for baptizing infants, does not envision that baptized candidates are being received during the same liturgy. The history of the combined rite for the Easter Vigil beginning at OCIA 562 will be explained below.

The conferral of sacraments upon newly catechized Catholics was new to the history of the Easter Vigil. It had no precedent before the 1974 Latin edition of the OCIA. The revisers apparently tried to make an appropriate accommodation for a particular pastoral situation that they detected among Catholics.

The same revisers envisioned a simpler process for baptized Christians of other denominations: suitable catechesis, no preliminary rites, and a ceremony of reception at Mass on any given day, not linked to the liturgical year, but to an occasion when the candidates were ready. The baptized adult Catholic, however, now fully catechized, could receive the sacraments of confirmation and Communion from a priest at the Easter Vigil, with permission of the bishop.

These same Catholics could join the neophytes in the period of mystagogy, participating fully at the relevant Masses of Easter Time (OCIA 410, see 247). However, this too is an anomaly in that one key point of reflection during mystagogy is the baptism recently received. Catholics of the group had been baptized some time ago, usually when they were infants. They would have no memory of the ceremony that mystagogy explores.

Other Christians as Candidates

Valid Baptism

To be considered a candidate, a Christian from another denomination needs a valid baptism, which can never be repeated. It perpetually changes people and makes them members of the Body of Christ.

Validity requires immersing the person into water three times, or pouring water over their head three times, while the minister recites the approved formula of words (c. 849, and *Catechism of the Catholic Church* 1239, 1278, and 1284). True water, not another liquid, must be used. Throwing water from a sprinkler does not accomplish baptism.

Some Christian denominations use the word "sprinkling" for what Catholics call "pouring." The minister pours a small but sufficient amount of water drops over the person's head. Some call this action sprinkling to distinguish it from immersion. If a Christian states that they were baptized by sprinkling, a parish minister does well to investigate a bit further. The method of baptizing may well have been what Catholics call pouring, and therefore would be valid.

Calling the person by name, the minister must use the assigned words: "N., I baptize you in the name of the Father, and of the Son, and of the Holy Spirit." These words may not be changed. The minister may not say, "We baptize you. . . ." Nor may the minister change the names of the Trinity to their function: "in the name of the Creator, and of the Redeemer, and of the Sanctifier." This holds to the church's belief that God reveals and enacts his plan of salvation "with intimately connected deeds and words."[1]

Additionally, the minister must have the intent of performing baptism. The minister need not personally adhere to Catholic belief, but must not intend something that the church does not hold. For example, the Mormons, with whom Catholics share many moral platforms, also perform baptisms using the same proper formula and gestures. However, their earnest understanding of the Trinity diverges so sharply from that of the Catholic Church that Catholics do not accept the validity of Mormon baptisms.

Many dioceses have published a list of individual denominations whose baptisms are considered invalid. The same list guides the process in marriage tribunals, where investigations pertaining to nullity depend partly upon the baptismal status of the divorced parties. To discern if a baptism is valid, one best consults a canon lawyer in the diocesan tribunal.

[1] Dicastery for the Doctrine of the Faith, *Gestis Verbisque* (On the Validity of the Sacraments), February 2, 2024, https://www.vatican.va/roman_curia/congregations/cfaith/documents/rc_ddf_doc_20240202_gestis-verbisque_en.html.

The mutually accepted validity of properly performed baptisms forges a strong ecumenical link among Christians. By honoring the valid baptisms of other denominations, the Catholic Church affirms its own doctrine on baptism as well as the foundational unity among Christians. This ecumenical sensitivity favors and celebrates the valid baptisms shared among various denominations.

Valid Confirmation

Catholics do not recognize the validity of confirmation in other denominations as broadly as they accept the validity of baptism. Many other Christian denominations offer their baptized members a ritual called "confirmation," which accomplishes much spiritual benefit, but it is not the same as confirmation in the Catholic Church. Catholic confirmation is one of the seven sacraments, a doctrine not held by many other Christians.

Furthermore, the sacrament of confirmation must be administered by a validly ordained bishop or priest, and the Catholic Church does not recognize the orders of other ecclesial communities. Consequently, if candidates for reception into the full communion of the Catholic Church have already been confirmed in their own denomination, they will likely receive the sacrament of confirmation at their reception.

As will be shown below, the Catholic Church does accept the validity of confirmation or chrismation administered in the Eastern Rites. Whether they are Orthodox or Catholic, they possess the same sacraments.

Catechetical Age

Some children of catechetical age have a valid baptism in another denomination. If they seek to be received into the Catholic Church with the approval of their parents, they are also considered candidates.

"Catechetical age" refers to the age at which a child may be personally prepared for sacraments such as baptism, confession, and First Communion. A priest who receives into the full communion of the Catholic Church one who is no longer an infant has the faculty to administer confirmation to that child (c. 883 §§1–2). A priest with this faculty must use it for the sake of the child's spiritual welfare (c. 885 §2).

Although canon law states this obligation in the strongest terms, one hears of countless cases in which priests have not complied by confirming children of catechetical age at their baptism or reception. For example, if these children have not yet reached the diocesan age for the confirmation of Catholic children, some priests think that they may not or should not confirm them. The law thinks otherwise. Such children are eligible for confirmation and deserve to receive its spiritual gifts as helps throughout the rest of their lives.

Sometimes parents present a younger child for reception into full communion. For example, the child may have been baptized as an infant in the non-Catholic Christian denomination of one parent and is still below catechetical age; now that parent is being received into the full communion of the church and wants the child also to be known as a Catholic. However, the liturgical Order of Reception has the candidates profess their belief in what the church teaches, and a child below catechetical age is incapable of owning and stating such faith.

The parents or guardians in this case may declare before the parish priest that the child is to be considered Catholic, and he then records the reception into the appropriate parish register, usually the baptismal register, where most people in the future would probably search for it. This constitutes a juridic act rather than a liturgical rite. A parish could issue a certificate of reception for the family to keep on file. The child would then receive preparation and the sacraments of confirmation and First Communion later, with other children the same age.

The Orthodox Church

Sometimes a person who belongs to an Eastern Orthodox Church wishes to become Catholic. "Nothing more is required of Eastern Christians coming to the fullness of Catholic communion, however, than what a simple profession of Catholic faith requires, even if, by virtue of recourse to the Apostolic See, a transfer to the Latin Rite is permitted to them" (OCIA 474). This directive cites the Second Vatican Council's Decree on Eastern Catholic Churches, *Orientalium Ecclesiarum*, numbers 25 and 4.

The OCIA affirms that any Orthodox person who becomes Catholic does not automatically become a member of the Latin Rite, the Rite that most Catholics in the United States experience in their parish church. "Latin" refers not to the language or to Latin America, but to the community of believers in the West usually bearing the shorthand "Catholic Church."

If a Latin Rite priest receives members of an Orthodox Church into the full communion of the Catholic Church, they become members of the parallel Eastern Catholic Rite. Their reception may take place in a Latin Rite parish, but it is more meaningfully celebrated in an Eastern Rite Catholic Church. This helps sustain the rich heritage of the East.

Once a person becomes a member of any Catholic Church, East or West, he or she may receive Communion in all other Catholic churches. For example, one becoming a Byzantine Rite Catholic may receive Communion in any Latin Rite parish church.

If the person from an Eastern Orthodox Church wishes to become a member of the Latin Rite Church, that requires permission of the Apostolic See. Such a transfer of membership can happen, but it is discouraged because of the value of participating fully in the Eastern Rites.

Almost every Orthodox Christian was confirmed at baptism, and the Catholic Church regards that chrismation as a valid sacrament. The Catholic Church recognizes the validity of the ordination of priests and bishops among the Orthodox. Consequently, a priest who receives Orthodox Christians into the full communion of the Catholic Church does not administer the sacrament of confirmation (OCIA 481, 493–94), which may only be received once.

It would be highly inappropriate for Orthodox Christians to participate in any of the preliminary rites for baptized candidates, such as the Calling to Continual Conversion or the Penitential Rite (Scrutiny). As only a simple profession of Catholic faith is required, they should not be included in events such as the diocesan Call to Continuing Conversion.

Rebaptism

Occasionally, someone will ask if they may be rebaptized. The Catholic Church does not permit another baptism of someone already validly baptized.

At times the person may stress that another baptism would better signify for them their reception into the church, but such a request signifies instead a lack of appreciation for what the church teaches about baptism. A baptism validly received is a grace beyond measure, and it sustains a person throughout their lives in all their spiritual journeys.

Temporary Residences

Special circumstances present themselves for candidates who have temporary residences apart from a normal neighborhood, such as those on a college campus or those who reside in prisons. More challenging is offering pastoral care to the unbaptized because their baptism is best celebrated during the Easter Vigil, a ceremony to which those in temporary residences may not have access. Those on college campuses may be baptized during the Easter Vigil at another place, such as a parish church; those in prisons may be baptized and confirmed at another time when a priest may enter their confines. However, for baptism of adults apart from the Easter Vigil or to use the Simpler Order of Adult Initiation, priests should consult their bishop, who decides whether, when, and how the rites may be celebrated outside the usual times (OCIA 34 §§2 and 4).

Those in temporary residences who have a valid baptism enjoy a more flexible formation and celebration. The priest may select their date of reception at any time of the liturgical year, in concert with the point at which their catechetical formation and willful desire are complete.

Irregular Marriages

If a candidate is in a canonically irregular marriage, the situation needs to be addressed before reception into the full communion of the church may take place. Such candidates fall into different categories.

For example, if the candidate's spouse is a Catholic, if their marriage was the first for both of them, if they were married outside the canonical form of marriage, and if there is no other impediment, then a priest or deacon may convalidate the marriage after suitable preparation. For example, a validly baptized Presbyterian woman wants to become Catholic. She had married a Catholic man in her own church, but he did not secure the proper dispensation from canonical form, rendering him ineligible for the Catholic sacraments such as Holy Communion. If this was the first marriage for both of them, they may request a Catholic ceremony to convalidate the marriage. (The Catholic would celebrate the sacrament of reconciliation beforehand.) This convalidation best takes place as soon as possible because it removes the irregularity affecting the Catholic party, who may then return to receiving Communion.

If a candidate is married to someone who is not Catholic, and if it was the first marriage for both, then the marriage is likely valid in the eyes of the Catholic Church, even if it took place outside a religious ceremony in a courthouse, for example. In that case, the marriage is not canonically irregular and no convalidation takes place. Other Christians are not held to the same canonical form as Catholics are for the validity of their marriage. They have a valid marriage and either of them is eligible for reception.

However, when a candidate for reception has been divorced and remarried, or has a spouse who has been divorced and remarried, then the diocesan marriage tribunal guides an investigation toward a potential decree of nullity on the earlier marriage(s). Such a decree makes the present marriage eligible for a convalidation, usually through a celebration of matrimony outside Mass.

Ordinarily, the sacrament of confirmation is to precede marriage (c. 1065 §1), and in some cultures, especially in Latin America, individual priests and bishops have *required* confirmation prior to marriage. However, in the case of a validly baptized Christian in an irregular marriage, that person is incapable of receiving sacraments until the irregular marriage situation has been resolved. Instead of the usual sequence of confirmation and then marriage, the convalidation of marriage must precede confirmation.

In 1983 the Congregation for the Doctrine of the Faith answered several questions about the eligibility of the divorced and remarried for Catholic sacraments. Some people erroneously think that a person in this category is ineligible only for Communion, but could receive baptism or confirmation. For example, a priest may think he could receive a divorced and remarried Baptist into the full communion of the church and administer confirmation, but withhold Communion. He may not. Asked if a divorced and remarried person could be admitted to baptism and confirmation, the congregation answered, "Our response would be negative."[2]

[2] Congregation for the Doctrine of the Faith, "A Response to Three Questions on Divorced and Remarried Catholics and the Admission to the Sacraments of Initiation," *Canon Law Digest* (July 11, 1983): 139–40.

Cohabitation

Occasionally a validly baptized person (or an unbaptized person) cohabiting with a Catholic fiancé before marriage asks to become Catholic. The *Catechism of the Catholic Church* considers sexual activity outside the marriage covenant gravely sinful and a scandal (2353). In truth, some engaged couples sustain a premarital sexual relationship without cohabitation; others share a residence but abstain from sex. There is a distinction between cohabitation and premarital sex.

A baptized person engaging in a sexual relationship prior to marriage does not demonstrate adherence to one of the church's important teachings and would therefore be morally incapable of reception into the Catholic Church. Their behavior is at odds with the spiritual life expected of members. The baptized candidate makes a choice: either sexual abstinence and reception into the church before marriage, which demonstrates the behavior the church advises, or reception into full communion after marriage, which may be more practical.

2

Elements of Formation

Team

Preparation for reception usually takes place within a parish setting where various elements may come together. The first of these is a director with a team to direct the efforts. The director is responsible for understanding the various stages of formation and how they apply to different people approaching the church for membership.

Catechists help candidates grasp the meaning of the faith and put it into practice. When the inquirers are unbaptized or have little knowledge of Christ, the best catechists are those skilled at evangelization and the basic questions of faith. In the case of baptized candidates, especially those who have lived a faithful Christian life, effective catechists will be especially conversant with the teachings that make the Catholic Church unique among other denominations.

A team may also include people gifted at praying and leading others in prayer. Often the catechists themselves have this gift. However, some people excel at praying more than teaching. They may provide their gifts to the group by sharing various forms of Catholic prayer, whether formal liturgies, such as the Mass and Liturgy of the Hours, or examples of popular devotion, such as the rosary, the divine mercy chaplet, and Stations of the Cross.

Others from the parish may have the gift of offering hospitality. Usually these are people who enjoy bringing friends to their home or hosting visitors. They often make good greeters at the doors of the church. At catechetical sessions, they may provide a warm welcome and refreshments to make visitors feel at home in a church that has attracted their interest.

Catholic sponsors may accompany the candidates (OCIA 483). Although that paragraph says a sponsor serves "if the situation warrants," a sponsor will be needed for confirmation, and the same person may accept both responsibilities.

Sponsors are often friends of the candidates—people whose lives have inspired them to learn more about the church. Those Catholic acquaintances make the most natural sponsors on a candidate's spiritual journey. However, the parish may also supply a sponsor for someone who has no such relationship. Many Catholics discover a recommitment to their own faith when they accept the privileged position of sponsoring someone exploring the same beliefs. Sponsors may need a coordinator who forms them for this ministry and helps out when catechetical or moral questions arise.

Eligibility for being a sponsor is the same as for being a godparent (c. 874). Candidates may choose their own, or a minister may appoint one, as long as the person has the ability and intention to serve as a sponsor. Sponsors must have reached their sixteenth birthday, but the local bishop or even the pastor may grant an exception for a just cause. The sponsor must be a Catholic who has received all three sacraments of initiation: baptism, confirmation, and Communion. Sponsors must also lead a life of faith in keeping with the duty they are called to fulfill. They must not be bound by any canonical penalty imposed by the church's law, and they may not be the father or mother of the candidate.

As at infant baptism, a single sponsor may be of either sex, no matter the sex of the child. At baptism two godparents may be used, in which case they must be male and female to imitate the role of the natural parents. Similarly, a baptized candidate could have two sponsors. In practice, most candidates have just one, probably because most candidates are adults who have matured into a different relationship with their parents, and the sponsor's role is less imitative of a parent's role.

Sometimes the parents of an infant to be baptized ask if a non-Catholic Christian may serve as godparent or sponsor. By canonical definition, such a person cannot be a sponsor but may serve as a Christian witness together with a Catholic sponsor. In theory, a baptized candidate could have both a Catholic sponsor and a non-Catholic Christian witness, but this would seem anomalous when the point of the ritual is to be received into the full communion of the Catholic Church. Indeed, the sponsor accompanies the candidate even for their formation and not just at their reception into the full communion of the church (OCIA 404).

When confirmation takes place during the reception, the OCIA calls the sponsor the "godparent" who places their right hand on the shoulder of the one newly received (494). As will be shown below, the term is copied from the Simpler Order of Adult Initiation, as well as *The Order of Confirmation*, which recommends that the baptismal godparent serve again as the confirmation sponsor (OConf 5). In the case of candidates, they may not have had a godparent at their baptism. If they did, it was most likely not a Catholic godparent, and therefore someone who would not meet the canonical requirements to serve as a Catholic sponsor. Therefore, the person fulfilling the role at the confirmation of candidates is most practically the sponsor who accompanies them during their formation and reception into full communion.

All those involved with the team are to keep current with the teachings of the church, as well as the resources available to candidates. This will help them work together and guide candidates to an untroubled life inside the community of Catholics.

Preliminary Conversation

To begin formation for reception, the candidate usually has an initial conversation with someone on the parish team. This dialogue will probe the working of the Holy Spirit already active in the person who has been baptized.

This conversation may take place in any setting—at someone's home or in a room on the parish grounds. Meeting at the parish ordinarily sets a better environment for the sharing of faith. In truth, the person could fill out a form online or have a conversation on the phone or by text. However, this spiritual conversation is best conducted in person, where the representative of the parish is fully, physically present.

The conversation unfolds as one Christian speaking with another. Both persons already have an experience of Christ. This differs from the preliminary conversation that a parish team member has with an unbaptized person, who is not yet part of the Body of Christ. The entire first part of the OCIA is dealing with the unbaptized. It concerns "Christian" initiation—not "Catholic" initiation. This wing of the OCIA respects the candidate's baptism, a sacrament of Christian initiation usually completed some years ago.

The preliminary conversation partly aims to discern if the optional preliminary rites of chapter V pertain to the candidate at all. The title of that chapter states that it concerns adults who "did not receive catechesis." In virtually every case, catechesis specific to Catholicism may be required, but chapter V deals with a situation comparable to those who have not been evangelized: they need Christian formation, not just Catholic formation.

Chapter VI, on the other hand, offers the Order of Reception into the Full Communion of the Catholic Church. It does not require all of the preliminary catechesis and rites that chapter V addresses. It respects the OCIA's position that no greater burden than necessary should be placed on those seeking the full communion of the church (473). Some candidates have extensive experience as disciples of Jesus Christ. This conversation will help chart their way forward.

Here are some questions that a catechist's preliminary conversation may explore with a candidate:

- "Who is Christ for you?" This question presumes that the baptized person has an acquaintance with Jesus Christ and has followed him. It aims to reveal how the life, death, and resurrection of Christ have shaped this person's beliefs and behavior. It forms a good starting point, getting right to the heart of shared Christian belief.
- "How did you come to know about Christ?" The person may respond by naming individuals who have influenced their faith, the religious habits that they have adopted, their experiences of worship, and their personal testimony of encountering the presence of Christ.
- "What are your favorite gospel accounts about Christ?" This question explores the extent of the candidate's familiarity with the life of Christ. It will build on their experience of communal and personal prayer, the preaching they have heard, and the meditations that they have practiced. By naming favorite passages, the candidate reveals the impact that specific accounts have made on their life.
- "Why do you think those particular passages stand out in your memory?" This may help both parties think about the candidate's spiritual journey—the personal challenges that they have faced and the sources of their peace.
- "How have you lived as a Christian?" This question presumes that the candidate has already lived as a disciple and can give examples. At home, at work, at school, even among strangers, Christians let their belief in Christ influence their activities. Some candidates may need help exploring this question, as they may not realize areas of their life that have expressed their religious belief; for example,

the care that they give to children, parents, or their own physical and spiritual health, or the jobs that they have held. They may come to a deeper realization how much they have already followed Christ, and how the upcoming steps will continue their practice of Christianity.

- "What Christian formation have you received?" Many candidates come with wide experience of formation, though some come with less. As children, they may have taken part in Sunday school classes, Vacation Bible School, family prayer, or personal study. Some have learned more about their faith in Bible-study groups or online chat portals. In the secular world, this question resembles filling out a transcript of previous education or compiling a resume when applying for a job. The goal here is different: the candidate is not trying to prove competency, but is rather helping the parish representative discern how to build on previous experience of life in Christ. Returning to the analogy of a formal education, credits transfer. Those who have learned about Christ and lived as his followers do not need the full program of initiation reserved for the unbaptized.

- "What experience have you had of Catholics?" Often a candidate becomes interested in Catholicism because of specific people. Good friends, coworkers, even a spouse may have opened their hearts to this expression of Christianity. Some candidates have not come to know many Catholics, but they may have heard about the church through impersonal connections or even a study of Christian history. Talking about their role models will uncover something about the values they hold and the desires they have.

- "What are you seeking?" This open-ended question allows the candidate to speak what is in their heart. They may seek community, a certain style of worship, or participation in the Eucharist. Some seek family unity, others want contact with more people who share their values. Knowing this will help the team make appropriate preparations for the candidate's formation. It may also reveal some of the disquieting circumstances of the candidate's life that have fed their yearning to deepen their life in Christ. These may require additional pastoral care.

- "What do you need?" This is related to the previous question, but it aims to hear from the candidate any specific requests that they have for their formation. Whether they need a better understanding of church teachings, seek peace of mind over aspects of church practice that have troubled them, or harbor concerns about their abilities to participate well, this question will help the parish team know how to accompany the candidate on this journey.
- "What is your marital status?" The Catholic Church takes marriage seriously, so a person's divorce and remarriage have an impact on one's ability to participate in the sacraments. The preliminary conversation needs to uncover this history so that the candidate knows from the beginning the church's vision of married life and its connection to worship. Although this may uncover challenges that need to be addressed with the diocesan marriage tribunal and require the sharing of much personal history, it will also disclose the value that Catholics place on the sacraments, a value that may have drawn the candidate this far into the process. For those candidates who are still in their first, faithful marriage, or who are still single, the church's teachings will affirm the longings of their heart.

Again, this conversation takes place between Christians. Both parties share in common something central to their lives: baptism. That supplies the foundation upon which the candidate's formation is built.

The Content of Catechesis

Reviewing OCIA 75

Formation for reception into the full communion of the church pertains not just to the mind but also to the heart and hands. The OCIA eloquently makes this point when it addresses the formation of the unbaptized during the period of the catechumenate (75). It envisions a fourfold process: appropriate catechesis, growing familiarity with the practice of the Christian life, suitable liturgical rites, and cooperation in evangelization.

These four processes presume that Catholics sustain their Christian life in the same ways. Candidates, therefore, may give evidence of these four organizational prongs from their past, while preparing to develop them further inside the Catholic Church.

Some of these questions may help the parish representative learn about the candidate's experience and focus their upcoming formation:

Concerning appropriate catechesis:

- How have you learned about Christianity in the past?
- Did you participate in Bible school or religious formation classes as a child? Were you ever active in Vacation Bible School?
- Did members of your family teach you about faith and morals? What did you learn?
- After high school, did you take any formal courses pertaining to religion?
- As an adult, how do you nourish your faith? What books have influenced you? What websites have provided inspiration?
- How have you observed the spiritual seasons of the year such as Christmas and Easter?

- Have you observed certain days, such as those devoted to St. Valentine, St. Patrick, Ash Wednesday, or Thanksgiving Day? Any others? How did you observe them?
- Has your religious formation been merely academic, or has it given you an inner experience of God?

Concerning the practice of the Christian life:

- How have you experienced communal prayer in the past? Was it with a particular congregation?
- How have you witnessed your faith to others? Can you give an example of a time when you made a decision based on your Christian beliefs?
- Jesus promised to come again. How has your expectation of his coming influenced you? Does belief in life after death change how you live today?
- As you go about your workday, what inspires you?
- How have you shown charity to your neighbor? What has it cost you personally to do that?
- Have you ever experienced disruption in relationships because of your decision to follow Christ?

Concerning suitable liturgical rites:

- Has regular Sunday worship been part of your life? Would you participate at Mass weekly as a Catholic?
- What memories do you have of worshiping with others? How has common prayer sustained you?
- In what contexts have you heard the proclamation of the Word of God? At church? On television?
- What similarities and differences have you noticed between Catholic worship and the common prayer of other Christian assemblies?

Concerning the apostolic life:

- How have you cooperated actively in evangelization?
- Have you shared your faith with children?
- How has the testimony of your life built up the church?
- What activities have required you to profess your faith?

Surprising to many, these four areas do not presume literacy. The idea for restoring a multi-staged formation to the Christian initiation of adults came from societies in Africa and Asia where not everyone could read, and where, even if they could, printed materials were scarce. Even the much-valued first prong, appropriate catechesis, does not require textbooks. In various other ways clergy, catechists, and other laypeople can present the church's dogmas and precepts connected to the mystery of salvation. They may do so in oral testimony, not only in reading assignments.

Consequently, the lived experience of Christians is itself a "textbook" worth opening. By reflecting on their own background, candidates learn more about the mysteries of Christ that they already hold dear, and they are led to a deeper sense of amazement in all that God has done.

Catechetical formation for candidates may build upon all four of these areas of the Christian life. Catechists who have learned about the experience that candidates bring can better focus the particular formation that they may need.

The Creed

The Nicene Creed is a key element of formation. At the Mass of their reception, the candidate will be asked to profess this Creed together with the gathered assembly. Appropriate formation, then, will include a review of this Creed line by line to ensure that those hoping to be received hold each of its tenets.

In the Roman Missal, the Order of Mass calls this more properly the "Niceno-Constantinopolitan Creed" (OM 19). OCIA 491 repeats this full title when it states that this profession of faith is always said at the Mass of reception. The tongue-twisting name of this Creed joins the adjectival forms of the two cities, Nicaea and Constantinople, whose councils in the fourth and fifth centuries crafted and refined these words. The common abbreviation "Nicene Creed" usually implies the full title and its extended beliefs.

The Nicene Creed elaborates the Apostles' Creed, which predates it, and which the Order of Mass calls baptismal and recommends for Lent and Easter (OM 19). An unfounded tradition holds that each of the twelve apostles submitted one line for it, thus providing its name.

The Apostles' Creed in turn reflects and expands the content of baptismal promises that predate it. Those to be baptized still make those promises, and the faithful renew them on special occasions such as the baptism of infants, the confirmation of previously baptized Catholics, and the Masses of Easter. These promises served as the source for the more elaborate Creeds and continue to distill their core teachings.

According to the Order of Mass, the Apostles' Creed connects best to Lent and Easter, the times of year when the elect are preparing to make their baptismal promises and when the faithful renew them. The Nicene Creed therefore appropriately fills out the rest of the year. It shows a more mature development in Christian thinking and more fittingly accompanies the reception of those who are already baptized and have grown in their belief and practice of the faith.

Here are some ways to make the tenets of the Nicene Creed part of the formation for candidates:

- "I believe." The first two words envelop a world of assumptions. The individual is making this statement personally. It declares one's stance. It resembles the making and repeating of baptismal promises. When asked, "Do you believe?" each person answers, "I do." The community of believers also holds these beliefs, but individuals compose the community, and each professes faith on their own. The tenets of the Creed cascade from the verb "believe." This word means more than an existential belief, as in, "I believe it will rain today," even when there is good evidence. It means more than "I believe that God exists." It implies trust, the centering of one's life. The words "I believe" begin this declaration of the organizing principles of one's life. Significantly, the Creed chooses the word "believe," not the word "know." A person has knowledge through the sciences, but a person has belief by looking past the sciences into their origin and purpose. Science and faith are not oppositional, but complementary.

- "one God." Before believers profess faith in the Trinity of Persons, they affirm the unity of the divinity. Christians do not believe in three gods, but in only one. Depending on the candidate's experience of Christianity, they may have a good grasp of this teaching. However, because of its centrality to Christian faith, it is always good to review what this means. See the *Catechism of the Catholic Church* (200–202).
- "the Father almighty, maker." Christians commonly call the First Person of the Trinity the Father. This follows the way that Jesus addressed the same Person in the gospels, and the term he permitted his followers to use when calling upon God in prayer. When Christians call God "Father," they are declaring themselves children of the same God, a title that they hold by reason of their baptism. This God is all-powerful and the creator of all things, of forces both visible and invisible, both in heaven and on earth. Orienting one's life toward this belief forms a confident foundation as one navigates the joys and stresses of the world. This belief also fosters care for the world that God created. See *Catechism* (232–421).

- "one Lord, Jesus Christ, born of the Father before all ages." Recalling the words of Paul (1 Cor 8:6), Christians believe that Jesus Christ is the one Lord through whom all things are and through whom they exist. He is therefore the eternal Son of the Father, truly God from God, as John proclaimed in the prologue to his gospel (1:1-3). He is eternally divine, retaining the same substance as the Father. As they come to know the gospels, Christians love to follow Christ because of the wisdom of his teachings and the awesome power of his miracles. However, his eternal divinity brought substance to his words and deeds. See *Catechism* (422–55).
- "he came down from heaven." As that eternal Son, Jesus was made incarnate by the action of the Holy Spirit and given birth by the Virgin Mary. This belief is so important to Catholics that they make a profound bow at Mass when reciting the words pertaining to his conception and birth. Twice a year at Mass, instead of bowing, Catholics genuflect at the same words: March 25, the solemnity of the angel Gabriel's annunciation of the Lord to the Virgin Mary, and on December 25, the solemnity of the birth of Jesus. The Creed proclaims that Jesus took on flesh for a single purpose: the salvation of humans. This section of the Creed is frequently criticized for its use of the word "men," which sounds as though Jesus came only to save males, and incongruously puts the phrase "for us men" into the mouths of faithful women in attendance. In Latin, the word for "men" here is gender inclusive, as is the Latin word a few lines later, where the Creed declares that Jesus "became man." The English translation strove to show that Jesus became exactly what he came to save: a man (that is, a human) to save men (that is, humans). But the point has been obscured, especially in the United States, where the word "men" is commonly heard as gender exclusive. Many people have no problem saying that the

second Person of the Trinity became "man" because Jesus of Nazareth was male. However, the Creed is not interested in his maleness, but rather in his humanity. A more accurate translation would say, "for us humans and for our salvation, he . . . became human." To some that sounds too biological, but it captures the intent of the Creed. See *Catechism* (456–570).

- "he was crucified." Having become human by his birth, Jesus endured human death—but not just any death. He died a cruel death imposed by enemies through suffering on a cross. The Creed stresses that Jesus died and was buried, and it makes this stark point before it proclaims his resurrection on the third day. To fully understand the resurrection, one has to grasp that Jesus actually died. Having ascended, Jesus sits at the right hand of the Father, and from that eternal throne will return as judge of the living and the dead. See *Catechism* (571–682).

- "the Holy Spirit." The third Person of the Trinity, the Holy Spirit, is also called Lord, a title more commonly assigned to the Father or the Son. The Spirit is also the giver of life, who proceeds from both the Father and the Son, and who spoke through prophets. As God, the Spirit receives equal adoration and glory with the Father and the Son. Candidates may share their understanding of the Holy Spirit, how they have heard of the Spirit's activity in the world, and how they have personally experienced the effects of the Holy Spirit. This may also prepare them to receive the sacrament of confirmation. See *Catechism* (683–747).

- "Church . . . Baptism . . . resurrection." The Creed closes with a series of beliefs consequent to those in the Trinity. The church is noted by four marks: one, holy, catholic, and apostolic. It thus shares in unity, sanctity, universality, and mission. Baptism forgives all sins and opens the door to the other sacraments of the church, as well as to the promise of sharing in the resurrection of Christ. Candidates may share their own understanding of "church" in the light of their baptism. Catechists may help them grasp the significance of their reception into the full communion of the church. See *Catechism* (748–1064).

- "Amen." The believer seals this litany of beliefs with the word that affirms prayers: *Amen*. Like the first two words of the Creed that introduce these teachings, this one concludes and adopts them all. See *Catechism* (1065).

Not all Christian churches have adopted the Niceno-Constantinopolitan Creed, but many candidates for reception may have been professing it since childhood. A review of its tenets leads candidates through a recollection of these points and the role that these beliefs have played in their lives, and it guides them toward their recommitment of faith in the Trinity and the church. A catechist fittingly reviews all these points with the candidates to ensure that each one's faith remains firm, that questions may be aired, and that a recommitment is appropriate, desirable, and timely.

"All That the Holy Catholic Church Believes"

At the Mass of reception, after candidates have recited the Creed together with the Catholic community, they immediately add these important words: "I believe and profess all that the holy Catholic Church believes, teaches, and proclaims as revealed by God" (OCIA 491). This translation differs slightly from the one previously in force: "I believe and profess all that the holy Catholic Church believes, teaches, and proclaims to be revealed by God" (RCIA 491). In one sense, the word "as" simply replaces the words "to be" to provide a simpler formula. Or this nuance could be intended: the church does not decide what God has revealed; God has already revealed the beliefs that the church proclaims.

This statement is meant to add the other principal beliefs that the Creed does not mention. Many Christian denominations hold the Nicene Creed in common, but not all hold other specific beliefs constitutive of Catholic thought. Perhaps the most obvious of these is belief in the Real Presence of Christ in the Eucharist. Another is the sanctity of human life from womb to tomb. Yet another is the divine inspiration of the Sacred Scriptures, a belief held by other Christians, but only implicit in the Creed, which relies on biblical testimony to expand its points.

The *Catechism of the Catholic Church* needs hundreds of pages to summarize all basic teachings. Candidates need not read the entire catechism, but it serves as a reference point for all the faithful in the universal church. The catechism or a derivative of it may have served as a textbook for candidates in formation. The statement denotes a general acceptance of the authority of the church, without enumerating these beliefs one by one.

In one sense, the statement resembles the box one checks when downloading an app to accept its legal terms. Very few people read all the terms, but everyone accepts them in order to reap the benefits of the app.

It also resembles the marriage covenant. At the wedding the couple agree to love each other for as long as they both shall live, but neither of them fully understands the details of the agreement.

All the teachings of the Creed are based on Sacred Scripture. Throughout the centuries the Catholic Church has reflected on the Scriptures in conversation with contemporary culture to apply the teachings of the Bible, and especially those of Christ, to daily life. To profess what the Catholic Church believes is to profess that the church has the authority to interpret and apply the Bible to contemporary circumstances.

Apart from the Bible and catechism, countless books, journals, and websites offer summaries of Catholic thought. As one would expect, many of these are reliable, though some are not. Authentic teaching can be found on the extensive pages of the Vatican's own website (https://www.vatican.va/content/vatican/en.html) and that of the United States Conference of Catholic Bishops (https://www.usccb.org). These deserve primary attention.

Those preparing candidates for reception best explore resources with a critical eye. The candidate probably already brings a wealth of knowledge about the Bible and is already discovering its application in the teachings that the catechism presents. These two principal resources will help critique other materials.

Preparation

Sessions

Catechetical sessions generally structure the preparation of candidates for reception. These may explore the teachings of the church so that the candidate can recite the Creed and subsequent statement of belief with confidence. However, one should not overlook the importance of other aspects of formation, such as participation in worship, service, community-building activities, and the evangelical mission of the church.

Although many people use the word "class" to describe the format of one of these catechetical sessions, the OCIA uses that word only once. It speaks about unbaptized children who may be enrolled in the same catechetical class as baptized children (298). Even the word "session" appears only once, in a footnote to a section about celebrations of the Word of God, added to the edition in the United States. There, it speaks of "instructional sessions" at which these celebrations may occur (89).

More commonly, the OCIA speaks of "preparation," a word that embraces many methods. It appears dozens of times in the book, beginning with the very first paragraph, and several more times in the General Introduction on Christian Initiation that precedes both orders of baptism, the one for children and the one for adults. Preparation may happen in many ways, even outside a classroom.

Joining with Catechumens

Such preparation may transpire at a place and time convenient to all those involved. In many parishes, the candidates participate in the same preparation as the catechumens. This is convenient, especially in parishes with limited resources. In practice, many leaders have discovered that all their inquirers have similar stories and questions, and that their hunger for the teachings of the church can be fed in the same way.

Catechumens and candidates often form a community among themselves, deriving mutual support from others on the same journey. All of this makes joint preparation defensible—up to a point.

In the end, the journeys of catechumens and candidates are different because the goals are different. One group is preparing to profess public belief in Christ leading to their baptism, whereas the other group is asking for reception while reaffirming their belief in Christ.

The timetables for preparation also diverge. Ordinarily, catechumens are preparing for baptism at an upcoming Easter Vigil. A candidate may be received into the full communion of the church at any time of year.

As noted above, the school-year model of preparation widely favored in the United States more aptly fits the needs of catechumens than of candidates. As students typically begin classes in late August and continue into May, so in parishes many adult catechetical groups follow the same plan. This timetable falsely assumes that all unbaptized people can begin their formation during the same month each year, even though some may feel the promptings of the Spirit at other times. Parishes best offer some flexibility to the unbaptized so that they may begin formation at different times, even though they are aiming for the same goal of baptism at an upcoming Easter—not necessarily the very next one.

The school-year timetable is even less fitting for candidates, who are not tied to Easter for their reception. Putting validly baptized people onto the same timetable as those who have not been baptized shows little appreciation for this reality. Many parishes design their preparation for catechumens and then ask candidates to fit in. However, a different timetable immediately results when parishes design preparation for their candidates, while asking the catechumens to fit in.

Individual Attention

The Order of Reception itself was composed for a single candidate, not for a group. See, for example, OCIA 489 through 498. The 1988 English translation used the plural form "candidates" near the beginning of this section, which fed the assumption that the priest receives an entire group at a time. The 2024 book accurately translates the assumption from the typical edition that the priest receives candidates individually.

However, the plural form remains in the combined rite for the Easter Vigil, OCIA 584–88, part of the innovations that first appeared in the 1988 edition for use in the United States. The original vision for the reception of baptized candidates is more accurately seen in the order of service within Mass beginning at OCIA 487, where the priest receives the candidates one by one, as each completes preparation.

The reception of baptized candidates may be celebrated more than once a year. It may take place, for example, at a parish Mass on a Sunday or weekday. The governing criterion for the reception of candidates is their readiness, not the liturgical year. Some people ask, "When is the appropriate time in the liturgical year to celebrate the Order of Reception?" That is like asking, "When is the appropriate time of the liturgical year for marriage?" It has nothing to do with the liturgical year. It has to do with the readiness of the candidates.

The OCIA in the United States permits reception during the Easter Vigil. However, it asks those responsible to apply theological and pastoral directives to the decision (562), even while calling reception at the Easter Vigil "a privileged opportunity to recall and affirm their own Baptism" (563). The decision to combine the rites is to be weighed against ecumenical values and guided by local conditions and family preferences (564).

Those choosing to arrange a formation of candidates closely parallel to that of the catechumens may therefore steer their reception toward the date of Easter. However, the Order of Reception does not bind the candidates to that occasion and is designed rather to be celebrated at another Mass at any time of year. Individual attention may guide candidates toward completion of formation and reception into full communion when they are ready.

Designing Preparation

Although the pool of adults interested in joining the church changes from year to year, many parishes report a larger number of candidates than catechumens. Yet not all parishes take advantage of this to design preparation for the greater number of those seeking membership.

The multi-staged catechumenate, ideal for advancing the unbaptized toward the waters of rebirth, is not required of the baptized candidate, and the lure of the liturgy entices many parishes to apply the same sequence of preparation and celebration to the candidate. In truth, the American edition of the OCIA contains rites for candidates that parallel those for catechumens, promoting a common timetable of formation and celebration. However, as indicated above, these adapted rites are for those who are uncatechized—those who received baptism but little other formation in the Christian way of life. They may be omitted.

Preparation for candidates need not last as long as it does for catechumens. Many candidates come with considerable experience and knowledge, and they benefit from a more focused period of preparation dealing with the particular concerns they bring. A parish may engage two or more separate groups of candidates each year, for example, conducting their reception as a group or as individuals.

Location, Frequency, Participants, and Length

The catechetical formation of candidates may take place at any location convenient to the group. Usually, a building associated with the parish makes the best choice, as suggested above for the preliminary conversation. Yet some parishes offer in-home formation at the residence of a catechist.

The pace of such sessions is usually weekly, but there is no required frequency for formation. Many parishes hold their preparation on a Sunday after Mass or on a consistent weeknight. The time can adjust to the convenience of those who meet.

Present for the preparation will be the candidates themselves as well as catechists or other team members guiding this part of the formation. If a sponsor has been chosen, that person's participation will enrich the gathering. However, the OCIA does not require the presence of sponsors. Priests and deacons have many responsibilities, but their participation at least from time to time will keep the candidates connected to parish leadership as a principle of unity. Depending on circumstances, candidates may share much of their formation with catechumens, who may also be in the room with their sponsors.

Candidates need not remain in the same preparation program for catechumens after they have been sufficiently prepared. The group is permeable. Some new members may join at any time, whether or not they have been baptized; candidates who are completing their formation may leave as they are ready to be received. Each candidate may need some individual time with a priest or team member to explore some aspect of the faith, to learn more about an area of difficulty, or to seek resolution for specific spiritual questions.

Structure

Preparation may begin with prayer focused on a passage from Scripture. Many use the Sunday Lectionary's selection of readings for guidance, but this is not required.

The fourth volume of the Lectionary offers additional inspiration. The readings there apply not to the liturgical year but to special occasions such as weddings and funerals. It also recommends readings for votive Masses and Masses for Various Needs and Occasions, grouped by theme.

For example, the fourth volume recommends readings for the Masses "For the Holy Church," which could form the basis for prayer throughout the time of formation (LM 827–31). These present a sweeping array of passages from both testaments, the book of Psalms, and the four gospels. These passages affirm the shared baptism of everyone in the room, which makes them all members of the Body of Christ and coheirs of the kingdom of God.

The section of readings in the Mass "For the Unity of Christians" (LM 867–71) receives special attention in the Order of Reception within Mass (OCIA 488). However, these may leave the impression that the reception of a baptized Christian is the exemplar of achieving Christian unity. Unity is not necessarily something that comes about as a result of someone becoming Catholic; it is a trait shared by those who are baptized.

After an opening prayer, the candidates may turn their attention to the catechetical topic of the day. Their preparation is to be both doctrinal and spiritual, "accommodated to individual cases" (477). In this way, candidates learn to adhere more lovingly to the church into whose fullness they will be received.

Many catechetical teams structure the topics for these sessions based on a curriculum reviewing the important teachings of the church. Others introduce more flexibility based on the specific needs of the group. Some individuals may need less of this comprehensive formation; others may need more. In selecting and presenting topics, catechists are to bear in mind this principle: "Equating candidates with catechumens is to be altogether avoided" (477).

Preparation may therefore include a formal presentation on some aspect of the faith, inspired by the liturgical year, the overall vision of formation, or the individual needs of members of the group. Effective adult faith formation combines teaching with conversation. Members of the group are encouraged to share their ideas and experiences, to ask relevant questions and contribute insights.

Plans for the coming week may come to light: service, socializing, learning, and praying. In this way candidates may put into practice the teachings of the church. They may plan these experiences as individuals or as a group.

Worship

Sharing worship with the Catholic community also forms candidates. This may already be happening according to the norms appearing in what OCIA 477 calls the Ecumenical Directory.

The 1972 typical edition was referring to the first such directory published in 1967 and 1970 under the title *Ad Totam Ecclesiam*. The Pontifical Council for Promoting Christian Unity revised that document and published its Directory for the Application of Principles and Norms on Ecumenism (DAPNE) in 1993. Therefore, OCIA 477 more appropriately refers to this updated directory. Its fourth section is "Communion of Life and Spiritual Activity Among the Baptized."

The directory promotes prayer in common between Catholics and other Christians. Together these believers put before God their shared needs and problems, including peace, mutual charity, family life, and the effects of poverty (DAPNE 108–9). Normally, other Christians participating in Catholic services do not share in the sacraments, as the directory explains (116–42). Still, candidates may have experienced some sharing in worship with Catholics before beginning their formation.

In addition to these formal opportunities for communal prayer, candidates develop their own private prayer life. They may also share prayer with others in the formation group when gathering for education or even just for the purposes of prayer.

Service

Faith demands action, and the candidates have probably already demonstrated their faith in various ways with their families and communities. Service is also part of formation.

Together as a group, the candidates may put their faith into action. They may volunteer for programs promoting social welfare. These may participate directly in a ministry of the parish or a neighborhood organization that the parish supports. Often overlooked as part of formation, service to others forms an important balance to doctrinal information and, indeed, expresses it.

Community Life

The candidates may participate in parish social life. They will gradually form new friendships with other worshipers and enjoy some recreational time together. This may happen spontaneously among individuals or more formally at parish gatherings.

These events build up the Body of Christ in love. They form the bonds that ultimately will be celebrated more fully in the sharing of sacramental communion.

Discernment

Discernment is a key component of any formation. In the preparation of the unbaptized, a discernment takes place before the Rite for Entrance into the Catechumenate (43) and the Rite of Election (119). These formal discernments examine the outward signs of internal conversion.

For guidance in discernment for the candidates, OCIA 477 calls for preparation that is doctrinal, spiritual, and liturgical. When members of the team make their discernment about a candidate's readiness for reception, they do well to examine exterior manifestations of the impact of this formation in each candidate, one by one.

Here are some questions that may assist the team's discernment:

- How has this candidate accepted the doctrines of the Catholic Church?
- Have we noticed any difficulties in their accepting what the church teaches?
- Do we consider these areas major? Have we attempted to resolve the conflicts? What were the results?
- Has the candidate manifested an understanding of doctrine by participating in sessions with questions, comments, and explanations?
- What differences have we noticed in the candidate's spiritual life throughout the time of formation?
- Is the candidate participating in common worship?
- Has the candidate spoken about personal spiritual growth?
- From what we can tell, is the candidate making prayer and spiritual reflection part of life?
- Is the candidate participating at Sunday Mass? Is attendance regular? What is the likelihood that the candidate

will continue to make Sunday Mass a priority after reception?

- Does the candidate have an appreciation for the sacraments of penance and Communion?

Mystagogy

Following reception, some new Catholics enjoy continued meetings with the team and the other candidates or catechumens remaining in formation for the sacraments. When meeting with the team apart from catechetical sessions, they may share the fruits that they experience from the sacrament of confirmation, and more importantly their new growth through regular reception of the Eucharist. New Catholics may also report on their engagements with other Catholics through prayer, service, and a sense of community.

The newly baptized are to spend the time after Easter in mystagogy, a period when they reflect on the sacraments they have received. This is not an academic reflection on the Eucharist, as may have happened during their formation. This is an experiential reflection. Now they are receiving the sacraments. They may discern their effects.

As mentioned above, the OCIA makes a case for uncatechized *Catholics* to prepare for confirmation and the Eucharist during Lent, along with the unbaptized elect (408–9). For the uncatechized Catholics, not only does Lent form a potential time for preparation, but the weeks of Easter offer a time for reflection on what happened (410).

The same paragraph does not directly apply to candidates baptized in other denominations, again because their reception may take place at a different time of year. Nonetheless, they may benefit from some reflection on the sacraments that they have received and the benefits that they have experienced, especially through their regular participation at Mass.

These questions may guide some conversations during this time:

- What did you experience at your reception into full communion? How did it feel to recite the Creed and declare your belief in what the Catholic Church teaches?
- What do you remember about your confirmation? What did you experience when you heard the list of gifts of the Holy Spirit? What do you remember about the imposition of hands? What struck you as you were anointed with chrism?
- Do you have an increased awareness of the Holy Spirit in your daily life? Have you noticed a specific growth in any of the gifts of the Spirit? Which ones? Under what circumstances?
- What do you recall about receiving communion with the Catholic community for the first time? How did it make you feel? In what ways has communion brought you closer to God? Closer to the community?
- In your daily life, have you put this communion into practice? Are you living the faith you profess by demonstrating that you are a disciple of Jesus Christ in communion with his church? How?

3

The Preliminary Rites

Reconciliation, Anointing, and Communion

Ecumenical Guidelines East and West

Christians baptized in other denominations are eligible for some sacraments in the Catholic Church if certain strict conditions pertain. Even those who are not candidates for reception into the church may be permitted to celebrate these sacraments on rare occasions.

Direction comes from the aforementioned Directory for the Application of Principles and Norms on Ecumenism (DAPNE). Available on the website of the Vatican's Dicastery for Promoting Christian Unity, this directory was published in 1993 during the pontificate of Pope St. John Paul II. It still provides guidance for many aspects of the Catholic Church's relationship with other Christians.

The section of this directory pertinent to candidates is called "Sharing in Sacramental Life, Especially the Eucharist," which contains two subsections, one concerning members of various Eastern Rite churches (DAPNE 122–28), and the second concerning Christians of other churches and ecclesial communities (129–36).

Regarding the Eastern churches, the Catholic Church holds that they have true sacraments, including the priesthood and the Eucharist (122). Catholics may participate in the sacraments of the Eastern churches except for those with more restrictive policies: Eastern Orthodox churches generally do not welcome Catholics to share the Eucharist.

Nonetheless, the Catholic Church does welcome Eastern Rite Christians to participate in all Catholic sacraments, including reconciliation, anointing, and communion (125). The Catholic Church would allow even the Eastern Orthodox to participate in Catholic sacraments on the theological grounds that the churches already share the same sacraments, but it discourages the practice out of respect for the more restrictive Orthodox preferences.

Latin Rite Catholics are not to practice proselytism, enticing members of the Eastern Rites to join a Rite of the West. The diversity of Rites strengthens the church, and members of the smaller Rites are encouraged to sustain their traditions.

Regarding Christians of churches and ecclesial communities of the West, the Catholic Church ordinarily restricts access to the sacraments. Such communities include those frequently grouped as Protestant churches. For the Catholic Church, the sacraments are signs of internal unity and a means of fostering unity. "Thus Eucharistic communion is inseparably linked to full ecclesial communion and its visible expression" (DAPNE 129).[1]

Nonetheless, any valid baptism in another denomination brings a person into a real though imperfect communion with the Catholic Church, and that baptism is directed toward acquiring the fullness of life in Christ. The directory draws this important conclusion:

> It is in the light of these two basic principles, which must always be taken into account together, that in general the

[1] Dicastery for Promoting Christian Unity, Directory for the Application of Principles and Norms on Ecumenism, http://www.christianunity.va/content/unitacristiani/en/documenti/testo-in-inglese.html.

> Catholic Church permits access to its Eucharistic communion and to the sacraments of penance and anointing of the sick, only to those who share its oneness in faith, worship and ecclesial life. For the same reasons, it also recognizes that in certain circumstances, by way of exception, and under certain conditions, access to these sacraments may be permitted, or even commended, for Christians of other Churches and ecclesial Communities. (129)

This paragraph cites several previous documents: the Second Vatican Council's Decree on Ecumenism, *Unitatis Redintegratio* (8); canon 884 §§1 and 4 from the Code of Canon Law; and canon 671 §§1 and 4 from the Code of Canons of the Eastern Churches. Again, this pertains to all Christians of other denominations, not just to candidates, who are indeed included.

Conditions for Sharing Sacraments

Several conditions have to be present, and then the proper authority needs to judge the true existence of these conditions. These are the conditions that DAPNE 131 outlines:

- The person does not have access to the desired sacrament from a minister of their own church or ecclesial community.
- The person asks for the sacrament on their own initiative.
- The person manifests Catholic faith in the sacrament.
- The person is properly disposed.

Ordinarily the diocesan bishop is to "establish general norms for judging situations of grave and pressing need and for verifying the conditions" (DAPNE 130). Ideally, he establishes these norms in consultation with the local competent authority of the church or ecclesial community in question.

Catholic ministers then administer penance, anointing, and eucharistic communion based on these norms, or, where the norms are absent, based on the principles of the directory.

If a person from another church or ecclesial community is in danger of death and fulfills the same four conditions, Catholic ministers may administer these sacraments on their own authority (DAPNE 130). For the sake of reconciliation and anointing, the priest makes the judgment. In the case of Communion, even an extraordinary minister of Holy Communion may do so. However, that minister needs to act cautiously in order to preserve all the values articulated in the directory: the general meaning of Holy Communion and the particular application of guidelines according to the circumstances.

The first of the conditions concerns limited access to a minister of one's own community. For example, this would pertain to believers living at a remote distance from the minister, who are imprisoned, or who cannot gain physical access to their minister due to health or work.

Thus, in the case of candidates in formation for reception into the full communion of the Catholic Church, they are eligible for these three sacraments under exceptional circumstances. One suffering a serious illness whose minister is unable to offer equivalent prayers for the sick may request anointing from a priest. One without access to Communion in their own church could make an appeal to the bishop for permission to receive the Catholic Eucharist. One seeking sacramental forgiveness could directly approach a priest.

However, the other conditions also need to apply.

- Is the candidate asking of their own initiative, without coercion from someone else, including a catechist?
- Does the candidate share Catholic faith in the sacrament, and how has this been evaluated?
- Is the candidate properly disposed through catechetical preparation and personal devotion?

- Is the candidate in danger of death?
- Are there diocesan norms, and have these been fulfilled?

As will be explained below, the OCIA expects that all candidates will celebrate the sacrament of reconciliation prior to their act of reception (482). The candidate may choose any priest and confess either anonymously or face-to-face.

Times of Year

The History of the Combined Rite at the Easter Vigil

As the revised rites of adult initiation spread throughout the United States in the 1980s and beyond, it became customary for baptized candidates to be received into the full communion of the church at the Easter Vigil. Catechists noted that their spiritual journeys were similar to those of the catechumens. Whether or not inquirers were baptized, all of them sought membership in the Catholic Church. The 1988 RCIA included a combined rite at the Easter Vigil to guide parishes through the sequence of prayers and actions that inserted the reception of Christians into a framework designed for the baptism of adults.

The first such combined rite appeared in the United States in 1977, just a few years after the 1974 provisional English translation, in a separate publication.[2] The typical edition in Latin, which had placed the Order of Reception in its appendix, had no such combined rite.

Preparations for the 1988 English translation in the United States sought to include the combined rite for the Easter Vigil into the main body of the RCIA. At first, the Vatican's Congregation for Divine Worship denied permission because of a position asserted by the Secretariat for Promoting Christian

[2] *The Reception of Baptized Christians and the Rite of Baptism During the Easter Vigil* (Washington, DC: National Conference of Catholic Bishops, Bishops' Committee on the Liturgy, 1977).

Unity. That group, sensitive to ecumenical concerns, feared that a combined rite would too readily group validly baptized Christians with the unbaptized elect, causing surprise and pain to other Christians.

To discourage combining the reception of baptized Christians with the baptism of the elect, the secretariat argued from several principles: the integrity of the Easter Vigil, the problems of inserting new elements into the rites of baptism and confirmation, the vision of the Order of Reception that permitted the Mass for the Unity of Christians and included the Nicene Creed, and the general introduction's declaration that the reception of baptized Christians should avoid any appearance of triumphalism, which a celebration at the Easter Vigil would surely violate.[3]

Ultimately, the Secretariat for Promoting Christian Unity begrudgingly approved a combined rite because those implementing the 1974 translation of the RCIA in the United States were already widely putting both groups together at the Easter Vigil in a liturgy of their own design. The secretariat felt it should take matters into its own hands and devise a celebration that would make the necessary distinctions between catechumens and candidates. The Congregation for Divine Worship then permitted the United States to publish the combined rites for the Easter Vigil in its 1988 translation. However, it requested that it be placed in an appendix, where it would appear to have lesser weight.[4]

The Combined Rite at the Easter Vigil in the OCIA

That explains why the combined rite still appears in an appendix to the OCIA. However, its location has made no difference. Those preparing the Easter Vigil in parishes turn to the

[3] Letter of Virgil Noe, Secretary CDW to Bishop Doyle, September 1, 1986, CDW prot. 432/86, cited in Paul Turner, *When Other Christians Become Catholic* (Collegeville, MN: Liturgical Press, 2007), 79–80.

[4] Turner, *When Other Christians Become Catholic*, 80–81.

part of the ritual book that they need. They have not viewed the appendix as a less desirable part of the book. Quite the contrary, they have put the appendix into widespread use.

The practice of receiving candidates at the Easter Vigil established an expectation for their catechetical plan and formation. The same appendix provides combined rites for the unbaptized and baptized at the beginning of their formation and in relation to the Rite of Election. Although the parallel rites for the baptized were designed only for those with little catechesis, the combined rites of preparation also gained widespread usage. Again, their appearance in the appendix made no impression on their desirability. These combined rites were among the elements that fostered the school-year model of formation for candidates, so that they would be prepared in conjunction with the catechumens.

The combined formation and combined rites also had the unintended effect of putting the Rite of Election onto the timetable of those who were validly baptized. In many dioceses throughout the United States and beyond, the parallel Rite of Calling the Candidates to Continuing Conversion for those who were already validly baptized has been frequently combined with the Rite of Election for catechumens, as if the validly baptized were all uncatechized and all in need of the bishop's assent before gaining access to eucharistic communion at their local parish.

This departed from the original, ecumenically sound vision of the reception of baptized Christians. Instead of clearing for them a straight path toward reception in their parish church at any time of year that they were ready, their formation became linked to the annual preparation of the unbaptized who passed through the cathedral in the presence of the bishop and then celebrated their initiation rites in parishes at the Easter Vigil.

The unbaptized generally celebrate their sacraments at Easter to show the connection among the themes of resurrection, spring, and baptism. But those who are baptized already share in the promise of resurrection. Their admission to the table is not universally required or universally appropriate at the Easter Vigil.

Rite of Welcoming the Candidates

Origins of the Preliminary Combined Rites

Justification for rites adapted for candidates comes from the typical edition itself. As noted above in the section on optional preliminary rites, the original Latin called for "liturgical actions, of which the first is a rite by which adults are received into the community and acknowledge that they have a share in it because they have already been signed with Baptism" (OCIA 405). However, the typical edition did not supply these. The American church did that for the 1988 translation, and they reappear in the revised.

Specifically, the typical edition aimed this remark to aid the preparation of uncatechized adult *Catholics* who anticipated a period of formation before receiving the sacraments of confirmation and the Eucharist. In the United States, the restructuring of elements in the English translation has drawn validly baptized Christians of other denominations into its reach.

These adapted rites all envision a group of candidates, rather than an individual one. As noted above, the typical edition envisioned the Order of Reception itself as a celebration for an individual candidate. The 1988 English translation imagined it as a celebration for several candidates in a single catechetical group. The preliminary rites composed in and for the United States all adopted the same view: several candidates attaining readiness for each stage at the same time.

OCIA 405 describes only the first of such liturgical actions, one of reception into the community and acknowledgment of baptismal status. It gave no further description of this liturgical action, nor a preference that it be modeled on the first rite for catechumens. A 1973 commentary on this paragraph from the

Congregation for Divine Worship can be seen in the appendix of this book.

This first liturgical action could have been a simple announcement during the introduction of some Sunday Mass. The celebrant could have informed the assembly about the presence of some individual Catholics who were beginning their formation for confirmation and First Communion. He could have invited welcoming applause and asked members of the regular assembly to issue words of support at a reception after Mass.

Instead, the edition in the United States created a liturgical rite based on the one expected for unbaptized inquirers. Furthermore, as indicated above, the original OCIA never called baptized but uncatechized Catholic adults "candidates." However, this adapted rite places them in that category together with those validly baptized in another denomination. This is made explicit by the sentence added to this paragraph only in the United States: "The Rite of Welcoming the Candidates, which follows in section A, is provided for this purpose" (405).

The revision of the subsequent paragraph (406) clears up a confusing choice of words from the previous translation. In 1988 this paragraph read, "Once a rite of reception has been celebrated, these adults take part in celebrations of the word of God." The revised edition reads, "From this time on they participate in celebrations of the Liturgy of the Word." The earlier translation used the word "reception" to refer to its rite of "welcoming," but "reception" is the name of the final step: reception into the full communion of the Catholic Church. The first step in the United States is called "welcoming."

Design

To describe those who qualify, the explanatory introduction to the Rite of Welcoming the Candidates removes one word from the 1988 edition. It used to say that the rite welcomes "previously uncatechized adults." Now it says it welcomes "uncatechized adults" (OCIA 411). This strengthens the point that the rite is not for all validly baptized Christians, but only for those who currently lack catechesis. If they previously lacked catechesis, then they are catechized, and this rite does not apply to them.

The very first words reinforce that this is an "optional rite." It is not required even of those who are uncatechized (411). OCIA 415 calls the rite "Welcoming the Candidates for the Sacraments of Confirmation and the Eucharist," which seems to refer to adult Catholics. However, it was designed in the United States for candidates for reception into the full communion of the Catholic Church. Their candidacy applies first to reception, and then to the sacraments.

The OCIA permits combining this rite with the Rite for Entrance into the Catechumenate (415, referencing 505–29). This fits a circumstance where the parish has both unbaptized persons and uncatechized candidates beginning this stage of formation at the same time. When describing the baptized, uncatechized adults in that version, the word "previously" has also been removed; the word "optional" is missing, but the Rite of Welcoming the Candidates remains optional (505). As will be seen, the combined rite poses some challenges, especially because its introduction requires careful distinction between catechumens and candidates (506).

The prayers and gestures of the Rite of Welcoming the Candidates are to acknowledge the validity and significance of the baptism that they have already received. The ritual aims to surround the candidates with care as they prepare for the sacraments of confirmation and Communion (412). Although not mentioned here, the rite also invites the candidates to express their intention, an act that elicits the community's care in the present. In some cases, their intention may actually have derived from the community's care in the past. Some candidates have decided to pursue reception because of the care they had already received from Catholics.

The only changes to OCIA 411 from the previous edition concern capitalization: official liturgical books now capitalize the names of sacraments such as "Baptism" and "Confirmation." The revised translation updates its schema for capitalization on these and other words throughout the OCIA, following the same principles that were put in force for the revised translation of the Roman Missal.

The rite is not linked to any time of the liturgical year, even when the parish plans to receive candidates at the Easter Vigil. Rather, local conditions determine the specified days (414). As with the parallel Rite for Entrance into the Catechumenate (18 §§3 and 44), this ceremony may take place several times a year as individuals begin their formation. This directive reinforces the view that the school-year model of formation has its flaws. Parishes are to welcome those interested in joining the church as the Spirit moves them to inquire.

Receiving the Candidates: Greeting

The rite spans two main parts: Receiving the Candidates and Liturgy of the Word. A note suggests that the celebration of the Eucharist may serve as a third part if the rite takes place within Mass.

As people gather, the candidates are to be seated in a prominent place among the faithful (416). This differs from the parallel Rite for Entrance into the Catechumenate, where the unbaptized gather outside the door of the church, at the entrance, some suitable part of the church, or even a suitable place outside the church (48). The very seating of the candidates acknowledges their baptismal status. They are not to be considered in the same spiritual category as the unbaptized.

When the candidates have taken their places in the nave, the entrance antiphon of the Mass or one of its alternatives may be sung (416). In the case of the unbaptized, the faithful may sing a psalm or hymn to begin. The entrance antiphon is not mentioned in the rite for the unbaptized because it more fittingly may take place apart from Mass, especially if the inquirers are unfamiliar with Christian worship.

In the combined rite that gathers those entering the catechumenate together with the candidates, the entire group meets outside the church (507). This logistical decision keeps the group physically in one place. However, OCIA 506 requests that organizers take care to distinguish catechumens from baptized candidates, and their common gathering place for this combined rite makes the distinction harder to see.

The title of this first part of the Rite of Welcoming the Candidates is now called "Receiving the Candidates" (416), whereas the former English translation called it "Welcoming the Candidates." The clarification demonstrates that the purpose of the rite, welcoming, comes later, not at the beginning when all arrive.

In the 1988 translation, the first part of the parallel rite for the unbaptized began with a section with the same title, "Receiving the Candidates," but here meaning those unbaptized persons who were candidates for entry into the catechumenate. Because of the potential confusion over the "candidates," the translation in the United States changes the word. For the unbaptized, the revised title for this section of their Rite for Entrance is "Rite of Introduction" (48), which more accurately translates what has always been there in Latin. The title that stands above OCIA 416, "Receiving the Candidates," which more clearly paralleled 48 in the previous translation, probably should have changed to "Rite of Introduction" if it aimed to show the connection to the rite for the unbaptized.

The hierarchical rank of the celebrant is unspecified (OCIA 417), but an ordained minister is presumed, as the combined rite makes clear (507). In the uncombined, parallel rite for the unbaptized, the celebrant is clearly a vested priest or a deacon (48). At his presiding, that Rite for Entrance bestows upon the inquirers the title "catechumens," who therefore obtain certain canonical rights in church law. In the rite for candidates, the celebrant will make the sign of the cross over them (422 and

423), a gesture reserved to priests and deacons. OCIA 423 mentions other priests or deacons signing the senses of the candidates, though catechists or sponsors may do so. A homily is to be given (427), and this is restricted to priests and deacons. Even though the Rite of Welcoming pertains to the baptized, has no canonical implications, is not required, and deals with a certain pastoral situation, the ceremony implies that the celebrant is a priest or deacon.

The celebrant greets the candidates warmly (417). No formula is specified, but he would appropriately use one from Mass, such as "The Lord be with you." The same instruction appears in the Rite for Entrance into the Catechumenate (49). In both rituals the celebrant addresses the entire assembly "pointing out the joy and happiness of the Church" (49 and 417). The celebrant is not simply reading words but engaging the community and acting in a way that demonstrates care.

By way of introduction, the celebrant may explain the path that led the candidates to this day (417). This explanation is also based on the one he may give concerning those about to become catechumens (49). Here, though, the rubric says that the candidates "seek the completion of their Christian initiation." For those baptized in other denominations, this is more precisely a path to reception into the full communion of the church, which will lead toward their confirmation and communion.

In the combined rite, the celebrant greets both groups warmly (508). The OCIA gives him a sample preliminary instruction to help all participants grasp what will take place. This instruction draws from several elements. It opens with words to the unbaptized, fulfilling the view of the preliminary instruction in the Rite for Entrance (49), and then it offers words of greeting to the candidates, fulfilling the view of the greeting in the Rite of Welcoming (417). Essentially the same as the greeting in the first English edition, OCIA 508 changes only a few words for the sake of internal consistency: "those who will be received into the order of catechumens" becomes "those who are entering the catechumenate," and "dear candidates," addressed to both groups, becomes "dear friends."

If the celebrant needs help formulating his greeting in the uncombined Rite of Welcoming, he could say words such as these:

> Dear friends,
> the church joyfully greets those who, already one with us by baptism,
> now wish (to be received into the full communion of the Catholic Church, and)
> to complete their Christian initiation through confirmation and the Eucharist.

He then invites sponsors and candidates forward. All may sing a suitable song, such as Psalm 63 (OCIA 417), which the combined rite also suggests (508). This copies the instruction from OCIA 49. The recommended psalm is more appropriate for the unbaptized, especially with its declaration that the one who seeks God is "like a dry, weary land without water." The adaptation in the United States makes no distinction between the baptized and unbaptized here, but in a parish setting, if a song is desired, it may focus on some other theme, such as the search for wisdom or fullness of communion.

As an alternative, one could draw the entrance antiphon from the first option of the Mass "For the Unity of Christians." It cites John 10:14-15, where Jesus proclaims himself the Good Shepherd. The third option from the same Mass offers another good possibility from Ephesians 4:4-6, where Paul affirms that there is one Lord, one faith, and one baptism.

Dialogue

The celebrant calls upon the individuals by name, or he asks for their names. This may be omitted if the names are known to those gathered. In a large group, he may ask only once, but each candidate is to reply individually. OCIA 418 offers a sample formula, but the celebrant may use other words. All answer individually, even if the celebrant asks the question once.

This dialogue is nearly the same as the one for the unbaptized in OCIA 50. However, in the case of the unbaptized, the celebrant may ask questions such as what they desire or why they have come. In the welcoming of candidates, only one sample question appears, "What do you ask of God's church?," which is also an option for the unbaptized, and which may be altered. For example, he could ask, "What do you ask of other members of God's church?," which would affirm that the candidate already has some share in the Body of Christ.

The sample response is unique to the Rite of Welcoming: the person asks to be accepted as a candidate for instruction leading to the sacraments of confirmation and Communion or "leading to Reception into the full communion of the Catholic Church" (418). The choice of words matters: a baptized, uncatechized Catholic only makes the request for sacraments and does not ask for reception into the communion of the church in which they are already a member.

The celebrant may permit the candidates to reply in their own words. As with the unbaptized, this opens a riveting opportunity for the candidates to share something about their faith with the gathered members of the local community.

Before this ritual, a catechist may take time during a session with the candidates to explore this question. What *do* they ask of the church? What do they ask of the church represented in this physically present, local community gathered around them? To prepare their response, the candidates may reflect on questions such as these in the days leading up this rite:

- What am I lacking that I believe this church will fulfill?
- (Or, for a Catholic:) After my baptism as a Catholic, what caused a delay in preparing and receiving confirmation and Communion? What has changed?
- What have I seen in this local community that I want to make part of my life?

- From my understanding of the sacrament of confirmation, what does it offer that will improve my future life?
- Why does the reception of Holy Communion appeal to me so much?
- What am I asking this particular local community to do?

As long as the candidates include their goal of the sacraments or reception into their reply, the answer that they share can inform the community how the members should help the candidates on their spiritual journey. Candidates may bring note cards or their cellular devices to read the remarks that they've prepared.

In the combined rite the celebrant questions the unbaptized first, and then the baptized candidates. The responses will help the gathered community distinguish the two groups (509).

The combined rite may continue with an exorcism and renunciation of false worship, but only at the discretion of the diocesan bishop (510). By implication, this would be rare, and it would only apply to the unbaptized entering the catechumenate (51), never to a baptized candidate.

The omission of this exorcism and renunciation underscores the power of baptism. Even though some baptized people have fallen into false worship, the enduring effects of their baptism make a prebaptismal exorcism nonviable and overpower the need for a formal renunciation. Indeed, the candidates will renew their baptismal promises—complete with the renunciation of all that is evil—on many other occasions: at every future Easter Vigil, when participating in the baptism of a child, or when receiving Holy Communion as viaticum at the end of their lives.

Candidates' Declaration of Intent

The celebrant poses a direct question leading to the candidates' declaration of intent. OCIA 419 gives the celebrant sample statements and questions for this purpose.

Throughout this section, the revised translation provides welcome sense lines for the ease of the celebrant. In 1988, an instruction like this appeared with words blocked into a single paragraph, stretching across the justified margins. Now the phrases are broken up line by line to assist proclamation. The usage of sense lines has long appeared in the Lectionary, helping all readers convey the meaning of the scriptural passage. Now, both here and elsewhere in the OCIA, the same technique is used. As a result, the celebrant runs less risk of losing his place, and he can nuance his voice more readily.

The first of these statements has the celebrant begin by quoting 1 Peter 1:3. This passage praises God who gave people new birth to a living hope through the resurrection of Jesus. The celebrant then applies the passage to the candidates before him, affirming their hope of glory through their own baptism. He asks if they are prepared to reflect, listen, pray, and serve, and the candidates declare their intent.

In the second option, the celebrant gives an open-ended invitation to the candidates to declare why they wish to take these steps. In this option, the declaration of intent is already implied in the celebrant's invitation; the candidates give reasons for the intent that has been presumed manifest.

If the celebrant wishes to improvise the question, he may use words similar to those provided. For example, he may formulate his words based on what he just heard the candidate say, especially if each candidate has given a unique response to the question, "What do you ask of God's church?" As the candidate is speaking, the celebrant may reflect on these questions:

- What am I hearing in this candidate's response?
- What does the church offer this person?
- What incident from the life of Christ does this bring to mind?
- What saying of Jesus responds to this need?

Then, the celebrant may improvise a response based on these reflections. He may begin with a reference to something in the New Testament—an action by Jesus or some articulation of the faith expressed in an epistle, for example. By repeating some of the candidate's own words, the celebrant may then connect the Scripture passage to show how Christ invites a deeper relationship with them. Then, the celebrant may formulate his direct question based on that reflection. He asks each candidate if they are prepared to continue their formation, building on the foundation of their baptism. In short, he may compose his question using this framework:

- Cite something from the New Testament.
- Connect it to the candidate's desires.
- Ask if the candidate is prepared to continue formation.

This section is based on material from OCIA 52, where the celebrant solicits an initial commitment from those wishing to enter the catechumenate. Although the structure is similar, the words show the distinction made for those who are previously baptized. Whereas the celebrant asks the unbaptized if they are prepared to follow Christ, he asks candidates if they will "reflect more deeply" on their baptism and pursue their formation. He presumes that the candidates already follow Christ.

In the combined rite, the celebrant addresses the unbaptized first. OCIA 511 supplies only one of three options for this dialogue from OCIA 52. When addressing the candidates (512), the celebrant uses an abbreviated form of the declaration and question from the Rite of Welcoming (419). Still, he uses these or similar words, so he has the freedom to alter, expand, or improvise the words supplied.

Affirmation by the Sponsors and the Assembly

The celebrant asks the sponsors and all the faithful to affirm their support (420). He addresses both groups together, as sponsors come from and represent the community at large.

This sample question is the same as the one from the 1988 translation. However, it is based on OCIA 53, which was updated for the present book. The differences are slight but probably should have been addressed in the revision. As the celebrant may use similar words, he could use these, more directly based on the rite for the unbaptized:

> You, the sponsors who are now presenting these men and women to us,
> and all of you brothers and sisters gathered here,
> are you prepared to help them complete their Christian initiation
> (or: prepare for reception into the full communion of the Catholic Church)?

All declare their readiness to help the candidates who are either completing their sacraments of initiation or preparing for reception. The celebrant adjusts his question to distinguish those individuals who were baptized in the Catholic Church from those baptized in another denomination who hope to be received into the full communion of the church.

In the combined rite, the celebrant addresses all the sponsors and all the faithful at once, making no distinction between those sponsoring the baptized or unbaptized (513). Unfortunately, the question is taken word for word from the Rite for Entrance, which asks the faithful to help the unbaptized to "find Christ and follow him" (53). Baptized candidates have already achieved that goal.

As the celebrant may use similar words to those provided, he may expand the question to acknowledge the unbaptized, the baptized Catholics, and those baptized in other denominations. For example, he could ask a question such as this of the sponsors and the assembly:

> Are you prepared to help them find Christ and follow him,
> to complete their Christian initiation,
> or to be received into the full communion of the Catholic Church?

Or the celebrant could formulate up to three separate questions addressed to each set of sponsors in turn. This would elicit the affirmation of the community for each of the groups standing before them.

The celebrant joins his hands and offers a prayer (420). Usually he prays with hands extended, but this gesture is copied from the instructions for a similar prayer for the unbaptized (53). The more reserved gesture of joined hands probably prepares for the action his hands will soon take, signing the individuals with the cross.

His prayer is copied from the 1988 translation, which was based on its presentation of a similar prayer for the unbaptized. If the intent was to echo that prayer, the 2024 edition could have offered another version of this one, updated to imitate its revised translation of the other prayer. For example, he could pray with words such as these:

> To you, most merciful Father,
> we give thanks for these your servants.
> You have already consecrated them in baptism
> and today they have answered your call
> to the fullness of the church's sacramental life in our presence.

Although the OCIA does not specifically give the celebrant the option of using other similar words to this prayer (420), the entire rite is optional, which implies some freedom.

In the combined rite, the celebrant offers the prayer prepared for the unbaptized (53), but says it over both groups (513). This prayer features aspects of fundamental evangelization—the human searching for God only to discover that God has already knocked at the door of the human heart. It is less appropriate for the candidates, who already have a relationship with God through their baptism. In context, the words have to apply also to those candidates who perceive God knocking a second time at the door of their heart.

One solution is for the celebrant to recite both prayers. Where OCIA 513 calls for only one, he could add the one for candidates (420).

At the conclusion of the prayer, the people are to repeat the celebrant's final line, "We praise and bless you, Lord" (420). This is more easily done in this rite than in others.

The 1988 translation copied the response for the people from the parallel rite for the unbaptized (53), but the 2024 translation slightly changed the celebrant's conclusion of that prayer, without altering the people's response. Now he says at the end of this prayer in the Rite for Entrance, "Therefore, we all praise and bless you, Lord," while the people are to respond, "We praise and bless you, Lord."

The slight variation between the celebrant's last line and the people's response faithfully translates the Latin original, but it adds to the difficulty from the people's perspective. In the combined rite, the conclusion of the prayer and the response of the people copy this variation from the Rite for Entrance.

The planners of this liturgy may consider offering practical assistance. Putting a prepared participation aid in the hands of the people, having the celebrant conclude the prayer with a simple chant, having a song-leader present, and fostering familiarity with this rite through repetition from year to year will all help the people make this response confidently and sincerely.

Signing of the Candidates with the Cross

The celebrant traces the sign of the cross onto the candidates (421). The heading that appears here, "Signing of the Candidates with the Cross," was found in the 1988 translation both here and in OCIA 54, where the word "candidates" referred to the unbaptized candidates for the catechumenate. The revised translation at 54 now carries the words "Signing of the Forehead and of the Senses." That revised heading probably should have copied over here for consistency.

The heading is a bit of a misnomer, even in Latin. After indicating the forehead, the celebrant authorizes the signing of other parts of the body. However, not all of these are truly senses. Furthermore, the words accompanying the signing of the lips have to do with speech, not taste. Even so, the heading refers to these body parts as senses.

The celebrant decides which senses are traced after the forehead and speaks the appropriate formulas (421). In the rite for the unbaptized, the diocesan bishop may authorize a different gesture in cultures where touching even the forehead may not seem proper (54). That permission is missing here for the baptized candidates, perhaps because the entire rite is optional.

Signing of the Forehead

The celebrant's introduction at OCIA 422 is based on one for the unbaptized (55B), which has a new translation. However, the words in 422 remain from the 1988 translation and do not account for the update. As the celebrant may use similar words, he may say something like this:

> Dear candidates,
> since you have expressed your desire
> to share fully in the life of the Catholic Church,
> together with your catechists and sponsors,
> I now sign you with the sign of Christ's cross.

The celebrant makes the sign of the cross over the entire group while reciting the words that pertain to the forehead. The catechists or sponsors trace the cross on the individual candidates.

This differs from the first option in the parallel rite for those entering the catechumenate. There, the celebrant personally traces the cross on the forehead of the individuals (55A). Instead, the rite for candidates adopts the gesture from the second option (55B), which has the celebrant making the sign over the entire group. He does so as a matter of convenience, because the second option confronts a situation where a large number of people are entering the catechumenate at one time.

In the case of the candidates, it appears that the celebrant makes the sign over the whole group because they have already been baptized. Still, the catechists or sponsors trace the cross individually on the forehead of each.

In the case of the unbaptized, this signing with the cross by the celebrant is a kind of branding that claims them for Christ. The Greek word *sphragis* appears in the New Testament to show that Christians have been signed or sealed in Christ (Eph 1:13 and 4:30). In this ritual, the same gesture is made on those already baptized, as a reminder of their baptism (422). The candidates have already been signed, sealed, and branded for Christ.

All may sing an acclamation (422). The recommended words are identical to those for the unbaptized and also serve as one of the options that replace the Alleluia at the gospel acclamation during Lent. The people may already know a musical setting and could enhance the ceremony with their song. Another acclamation may be sung, but the planners best choose one that is addressed to Christ, not to the candidates.

Signing of the Other Senses

The celebrant may continue with the signing of other body parts: ears, eyes, lips, chest, shoulders, hands, and feet (423). This section copies the material for the signing of the unbaptized (56), once again making little distinction between the two groups. Priests or deacons may assist in the signing, as may be done with the unbaptized. Because these signings are optional, and because the candidates have already been baptized, it may be ecumenically sensitive to opt out of this part of the ritual. Still, it is permitted.

The celebrant makes a final sign of the cross over all the candidates, imitating the gesture he would make over the unbaptized (423 and 56). He then concludes with the collect from the Mass of the day or with a prayer proper to the occasion (424). That one is based on OCIA 57B and reflects the revised translation of that prayer.

The option for offering the collect appears here, but not in the parallel Rite for Entrance (57). As noted above in consideration of the missing entrance antiphon, this suggests that those becoming catechumens, because they have never been baptized, may not celebrate this rite during Mass. However, the candidates, because of their baptism and in spite of their lack of catechesis, more likely celebrate this rite at the start of Mass. In that case, the collect occurs here. If celebrated on a Sunday or another day when the Gloria is normally said or sung, the rubric is not clear. Perhaps, in light of the solemn day, it is still sung, as for weddings and the baptisms of children at Mass. Or perhaps, absent any other direction here, it is to be omitted since this celebration is not yet that of a sacrament.

The Combined Rite: Signings

In the combined rite, the celebrant first signs those entering the catechumenate. The rubrics of OCIA 54 and 55 are lightly rewritten in 514 and 515 to make clear which group goes first.

The celebrant has two options for the invitation and signing of the forehead of those entering the catechumenate (55), but only the first appears in the combined rite (515). His words for signing the senses in OCIA 516 are copied from OCIA 56.

The celebrant then turns to sign the candidates, as the heading of this section makes clear (518). OCIA 517 and 518 copy the material from 421 and 422. In the combined rite, the celebrant addresses the candidates by name when signing their forehead (518), though he does not call them by name in the uncombined rite (422). The discrepancy is probably an editorial oversight. As the person's name is not included in the Rite for Entrance (55B), nor when signing the unbaptized in the combined rite (516), it probably does not belong in 518.

The prayer that concludes both sets of signings (520) is the second option for those becoming catechumens (57B), which implies that all these servants are now being signed with the cross of Christ for the first time. It is less appropriate for the candidates. The collect of the day may replace this prayer in the uncombined rite for the candidates (424), but that option is not mentioned here. If this ceremony takes place during Mass, the collect for the day would appropriately substitute for the prayer at 520.

For catechumens, at the conclusion of this prayer in their Rite for Entrance, they may each be presented with a cross of Christ to keep (59). Alternatively, as will be seen, they may receive the cross at the time of the presentation of the gospels (64). The combined rite refers to both alternatives at 525, but it overlooked mentioning the first option at 520. If a cross is to be presented to catechumens in the combined rite, the action may take place after the prayer that concludes the signings.

The OCIA does not offer the option of presenting a cross to the candidates—neither in their Rite of Welcoming nor in the combined rite. This suggests that they already belong to Christ.

The Combined Rite: Introduction into the Church

Also in the combined rite, the introduction into the church building, which comes exclusively from the Rite for Entrance for the unbaptized, is inserted into the Rite of Welcoming because the baptized candidates have been made to gather outside the church together with the unbaptized (521, see 60). Those previously baptized are also invited to come into the church to partake at the table of God's word, as if they had never had this opportunity before. This unfortunate practical necessity blurs the difference between catechumens and candidates. It can be avoided by leaving the rites uncombined, celebrating them at different Masses or different days, or by omitting the Rite of Welcoming the Candidates.

At the combined rite, at the church door or wherever the rite has thus far taken place, the celebrant gestures for both groups to enter, another rubric borrowed from the rite for those anticipating baptism. This is all that remains of a rubric in the pre–Vatican II order of baptism of adults, when the priest used his left hand to hold the right wrist of the adult to be baptized (or offered the left side of the stole hanging around his shoulders to the person's right hand). He then led the person into the church. If there were several adults to be baptized, they similarly joined hands in a kind of daisy chain for this procession (*Rituale Romanum: Ordo Baptismi Adultorum* 29). Today the priest may more simply hold open the door to the church or make some other gesture of invitation. Again, it is unfortunate that the combined rite, out of an apparent concern for logistics, puts the baptized candidates in this situation.

The recommended music selects verses from Psalm 34 with an antiphon inviting those entering to learn the fear of the Lord. The verses include a blessing over those who seek the Lord. This recommendation comes from the Rite for Entrance for those who have just become catechumens through the signings of the cross (60). Even the music treats the candidates like catechumens.

Liturgy of the Word: Instruction

In the uncombined Rite of Welcoming the Candidates, before the readings begin, the celebrant addresses the candidates and the sponsors to help them "understand the dignity of God's word, which is proclaimed and heard in the church" (425). In the combined rite, he gives the same address to both catechumens and candidates (522).

This description comes from the rite for the catechumens, which notes that those who began the celebration outside the front door or in another place apart from the nave now reached their seats inside the church for the first time (61). In the uncombined rite, the candidates begin the ceremony inside because they have already been baptized. Reaching their seats at this point is not one of the symbols appropriate for candidates, but in the combined rite, they comply to do so together with those who are unbaptized.

The very existence of the celebrant's introduction to the Liturgy of the Word lends more evidence that this rite is intended for candidates who have had little or no catechesis. The celebrant has to explain what God's word is and how it is used in church. Many previously baptized candidates do not need such rudimentary instruction, nor this rite.

Readings

The readings of the day are recommended, but others may be chosen "according to the norms of the Lectionary" (426). Actually, the norms are more clearly expressed in the Missal. Ritual Masses "are prohibited on Sundays of Advent, Lent, and Easter, on Solemnities, on the days within the Octave of Easter, on the Commemoration of All the Faithful Departed (All Souls' Day), on Ash Wednesday, and during Holy Week" (GIRM 372). Proclaiming readings other than those assigned for the day is prohibited on those occasions.

The combined rite suggests the readings appropriate to catechumens, though it permits other appropriate passages (OCIA 523). Indeed, the Rite for Entrance into the Catechumenate has its own set of recommended readings (62). These, which pertain to God's call, are more fitting for those who are discerning whether to follow Christ for the first time. They are not appropriate for those who have been baptized. This shows the difficulty of finding readings appropriate to both groups, except perhaps the readings of the day.

Homily

The homily "explains the readings" (427), a slightly more elaborate description than the instruction in the rite for catechumens, which simply states "The Homily follows" (63). Usually a homily is based on the readings, but GIRM 65 permits a homily based on another text from the Mass of the day. The option is rarely taken, but the Order of Mass and the presidential prayers offer a more expansive treasure of sources for preaching. The difference in description of the homilies was probably not intended. The 1988 translation said also in the rite for catechumens that the homily explains the readings (63). The 2024 revision gives a more accurate translation at 63 but failed to update the wording at 427. The combined rite adopts the more ample description from the rite for candidates (524).

The homilist is not specified. By its nature, the homily at Mass is never given by a layperson, but only by a priest or deacon (GIRM 66). The celebrant of this rite or another priest or deacon present is the logical homilist. The same applies to the combined rite.

Presentation of the Gospels

The presentation of the gospels is optional (OCIA 428). In the rite for catechumens, a book containing the gospels and even a cross may be given (64). As noted above, for candidates, the option of receiving the cross is not offered, probably to acknowledge the baptism that they have already received. The presentation of the gospels signifies catechetical formation that they have *not* received. Baptized candidates who have already formed their lives on the gospels would not appropriately receive a Book of the Gospels at this time.

The book in question could be the entire Bible, but more appropriately a publication of the four gospels alone. Some publishers offer such a collection in a slim volume together with the book of Psalms. The OCIA probably does not intend the presentation of the parish's Book of the Gospels, which a deacon or reader may carry in procession and place on the altar at the beginning of Sunday Mass. That book contains excerpts arranged for the liturgical year, rather than the complete text of all four gospels.

The rite does not say who distributes the book of Scriptures to the candidates. Besides the celebrant, this could be a catechist, sponsor, or a deacon, whose ministry includes proclaiming the gospel. Nonetheless, the last words of OCIA 428 indicate that the book is a gift of the celebrant. The celebrant recites a formula, so even if someone else passes out the books, the celebrant makes the oral gift.

The celebrant may speak the sample statement proposed in 428, which invites the candidate to receive the gospel of Jesus Christ. However, he may prepare or improvise another formula. This formula suggests that the candidates, though baptized, are so uncatechized that they have not yet encountered the gospel of Christ. It may or may not be fitting.

The candidate may respond with appropriate words (428). These may be words of thanks to the celebrant or to God, for example. The candidate may prepare these ahead of time or speak spontaneously. Before the celebration, catechists could help the candidates prepare a response with questions such as these:

- What gospel passages have struck you the most?
- How do you see the role of the gospels in your upcoming formation?
- If you could say something to God about the four gospels, what would it be? Why?

In the combined rite, both the catechumens and the candidates receive the presentation of the gospels. No distinction is made, though one could be made by presenting the books only to the unbaptized.

Also in the combined rite, the catechumens alone may be given a cross if they did not receive one earlier in this rite (525, which permits the alternative time for the presentation after the prayer at 520, though the citation is missing there).

In the combined rite celebrated at a Mass, the catechumens may be dismissed (528). This is the preference if the gathering continues with the Liturgy of the Eucharist, but it is not obligatory.

The OCIA never calls for the dismissal of baptized candidates after the homily, as it recommends for catechumens (67). Even though the candidates may not yet share at the eucharistic table, they may fittingly take part in the succeeding elements proper to Christians: the Creed, the universal prayer, the preparation of the gifts, the eucharistic prayer, the Lord's Prayer, and the sign of peace. The unbaptized may be present for these parts of the Mass, but their status renders them less capable to fulfill them than those who have been baptized.

Profession of Faith

The Creed is said when the liturgical day calls for it (429). For example, if this ceremony takes place during Mass on a Sunday or solemnity, all recite the Creed together.

The Creed anticipates an important upcoming event. The candidates will recite it solemnly on the day of their reception.

Universal Prayer (Prayer of the Faithful)

The universal prayer is the prayer *of the faithful*. That is, it is part of the responsibility of the baptized priestly people, as explained in GIRM 69.

When the parallel rite for catechumens takes place at Mass, the intercessions may be divided. The first set focuses on the catechumens, who may then be dismissed before the faithful continue with the second set of petitions "for the needs of the Church and of the whole world" (OCIA 65).

However, in Mass with the candidates, there is no dismissal and no division of the petitions. The intentions for the candidates are added to those for the church and the world (430).

In the combined rite, the intercessions precede the Creed because of the potential dismissal of the catechumens. In that case, the catechumens are present for the first set of intentions, and the second set comes after their dismissal. Alternatively, all the petitions may be offered before the dismissal of the catechumens, including those for the church and the world. In that case, after the Creed, the universal prayer is omitted (526). More accurately, it has already been absorbed into the earlier prayer. Ideally, the division of these petitions is honored, so that the catechumens are present only for those that pertain to them, and the candidates join the rest of the baptized community, exercising the duty of their baptismal priesthood by praying for the church and the world.

The OCIA calls the person who leads the petitions in both instances the "lector." The previous translation called this an "assisting minister."

GIRM 101 distinguishes between a lector formally instituted by a bishop and another reader more commonly deputed to assist when no instituted lector is present. In the past, the ministry of lector was reserved to males and in practice the bishop instituted into this ministry only those men who were candidates for the diaconate and priesthood. A bishop may now institute women as lectors if they fulfill the spiritual, catechetical, and gubernatorial qualifications for this ministry. More commonly, parishes have "readers" whom the priest asks to fulfill the duty.

The Latin original of OCIA 65 indeed uses the word "lector," a minister whom few parishes have. However, the same Latin word appears in the GIRM for both instituted lectors and deputed readers (116, for example). The choice of the word in the

OCIA therefore allows the use of a non-instituted reader. Yet, if a deacon is present, the reading of the petitions more properly falls to him (GIRM 71).

The OCIA offers no sample introduction for these petitions (430) as it does for new catechumens. There the celebrant recruits the joy-filled spirit of the assembly to pray that the catechumens may complete the journey that awaits them "toward full participation in our way of life" (65).

The celebrant may improvise his own introduction, which probably should focus more on the universal needs of the church and world than on the particular needs of the candidates. After all, as baptized members of the community, they stand with the Catholic faithful in offering these petitions together. For example, the celebrant could introduce the petitions with words such as these:

> These candidates, our brothers and sisters,
> have already traveled far.
> We rejoice with them in the gentle guidance of God, which
> has brought them to this day.
> We invite them to pray with us
> for the needs of the church and the world.

The sample petitions are focused on the candidates, but with the instruction that only "one or more" be added to the other intentions (430). These are based on the petitions for the catechumens. The revised translation has lightly edited those from the 1988 translation, and has aligned them more closely to those for catechumens in OCIA 65.

Both sets share some petitions in common, but in place of prayers that the catechumens embrace "the entire will of God" and enjoy the "sincere and unfailing support" of the faithful on their journey (65), these petitions ask that the candidates receive "a deeper appreciation of the gift of their Baptism" (430). The final petition for catechumens prays that they be found worthy of baptism, whereas the one for the candidates prays that they be sealed with confirmation and come to the table of Communion.

One phrase is optional in that final petition, that these candidates be "embraced by the Father's merciful forgiveness" (430). This seems to refer to those validly baptized in other Christian communities, praying that they repent, but not that the Catholic candidates do so. If so, the retention of that phrase in the revision is an unfortunate oversight. The Second Vatican Council's Decree on Ecumenism said plainly, "The children who are born into these Communities and who grow up believing in Christ cannot be accused of the sin involved in the separation, and the Catholic Church embraces upon them as brothers, with respect and affection" (3).[5]

Again, the OCIA envisions that not all of these petitions are used in the Rite of Welcoming. Only one or more is added to the regular petitions of the day.

In the combined rite, the petitions are drawn completely from those prepared for the unbaptized catechumens. The introduction is the same as the one from the Rite for Entrance into the Catechumenate (65), but it adds the candidates among those for whom the community is praying. A more nuanced introduction could be used:

> These catechumens and candidates, our brothers and sisters,
> have already traveled far.
> We rejoice with them in the gentle guidance of God,
> which has brought them to this day.
> Together let us pray especially for these catechumens,
> that they may have the strength to complete the great journey
>   that lies ahead
> toward full participation in our way of life.

[5] *Unitatis Redintegratio* (Decree on Ecumenism), November 21, 1964, https://www.vatican.va/archive/hist_councils/ii_vatican_council/documents/vat-ii_decree_19641121_unitatis-redintegratio_en.html.

The final petition expands to include the sacramental goals of the candidates, distinct from that of catechumens (526). The sensitive wording of this intention sets a good example of how to pray for these individuals.

These intercessions may be replaced by other similar ones, so the local community has the option of emending these even further. However, if the catechumens are to be dismissed next, before the prayer of the faithful, it would be appropriate to focus these petitions on their needs.

Concluding Prayer

In the uncombined Rite of Welcoming, a prayer concludes the petitions (431). In the 1988 translation, it was called "Prayer over the Candidates." Now it is more properly called "Concluding Prayer," the same title as the parallel prayer for catechumens (66). The celebrant is instructed to use this prayer, rather than an improvised one, as is typically the case.

The prayer is the same as the one in the former translation, a creation for the Catholic Church in the United States with no equivalent in the typical edition. One could argue that a concluding prayer to these petitions more fittingly addresses universal needs, not the needs of the candidates. Nonetheless, the prayers of the entire gathered assembly of the faithful turn once again toward those among them who are preparing for reception and for the sacraments of confirmation and Communion.

In the combined rite, the concluding prayer is taken from the rite for the unbaptized (66B). It prays that both groups "be made new" and attain "complete conformity" with Christ (527). However, the candidates already enjoy those fruits by reason of their baptism. Because the candidates have been baptized and thus have the competency for offering the prayer of the faithful, the celebrant could amend this prayer to underscore that the focus of the petitions has been on the unbaptized.

For example, instead of praying "welcome these beloved ones who have taken this step," he could say, "welcome these beloved catechumens who have taken this step."

Dismissal of the Assembly

If the Liturgy of the Eucharist does not continue, then an appropriate song may be sung, and all are dismissed together (432, 528D). In the combined rite, the catechumens may be dismissed, though not the candidates (528AB). Nonetheless, if necessary, the catechumens may receive an invitation to remain (528C).

The 1988 translation assigned the words of dismissal to the celebrant. In the revised, the minister who issues the dismissal at the Rite of Welcoming is not indicated (430). The combined rite copies the permission from the rite for the unbaptized (67ABC), which allows either a deacon or a priest to speak these words (528ABC). If a deacon is present, he would more fittingly take this responsibility.

The 1988 translation concluded the dismissal formula with the word "always," as in, "may the Lord remain with you always." Throughout the OCIA this word has been removed from the dismissals of the 2024 translation simply because it has no equivalent in Latin. Indeed, the dismissal is more focused on the present needs, not perpetual ones. The combined rite now concludes the same way (528D).

Celebration of the Eucharist

The universal prayer may be omitted or added—omitted probably if it seems repetitious, added so that the candidates may join other members of the faithful in offering prayer for the universal needs of the church and the world. The Creed follows when it is required (529), as when this rite takes place within Sunday Mass. This reverses the order of these two elements of the Mass, but the same applies to other rites, such as matrimony within a Sunday Mass, where the petitions conclude the wedding proper, so the Creed is displaced to avoid an interruption (*The Order of Celebrating Matrimony* 69).

When the uncombined Rite of Welcoming the Candidates takes place during Mass, the preparation of the gifts opens the Liturgy of the Eucharist (433). The rest of the celebration continues as usual. The heading here and in the combined rite reads "Celebration of the Eucharist," but it is more accurately "The Liturgy of the Eucharist," as reads the heading in the Order of Mass 21. The celebration of the Eucharist has already begun.

Common Prayer after the Rite of Welcoming

After their Rite of Welcoming, the candidates are to take part regularly in Sunday Mass and in celebrations of the Word of God—those celebrated with all Christians and those arranged for the candidates (OCIA 413). Participation at Mass is the first recommendation, where the candidates will hear the Word of God in the context of the liturgy and deepen their habit of Sunday worship. The 2024 translation changes 1988's "Sunday eucharist" to "Sunday Mass," which is the title that the Roman Missal gives this weekly gathering.

Regarding the other prayer opportunities, OCIA 413, which was composed in the United States for all candidates, refers back to 406, which originally encouraged baptized, uncatechized adult *Catholics* to participate in Liturgies of the Word. Those Catholics may gather for such prayer with "the group of the faithful," meaning experienced Catholics, or on their own, as catechumens may do.

OCIA 413 echoes this plan when it distinguishes two types of "Celebrations of the Word of God"—one "in the full Christian assembly" and the other arranged for the candidates. In the first of these, the 2024 translation repeats an imprecision from 1988. Referring back to the recommendation for uncatechized, baptized Catholics (406), OCIA 413 offers celebrations with "the entire Christian assembly," which appeared to promote ecumenical prayer. The revision of 406 more correctly states the OCIA's intent: the first option for celebrations of the Liturgy of the Word is with "the group of the faithful," meaning the Catholic community.

The revised translation probably should have corrected OCIA 413 to imitate the words in 406 in this way: Candidates may "participate in celebrations of the Liturgy of the Word, both those at which the group of the faithful is gathered and those that are designed in a similar way for candidates." That would have clarified the link to 406, as well as the intent to foster their formation among the Catholic community. Prayer with other Christians is always praiseworthy, but these paragraphs pertain to other gatherings.

In summary, candidates may participate at Sunday Mass or in a Liturgy of the Word apart from Mass. That may be a liturgy that gathers the Catholic faithful or a prayer service designed especially for them.

Handing On of the Creed

The Rites of Handing On

OCIA 407 permits baptized, uncatechized candidates to participate in the Rites of Handing On, which traditionally belong only to the unbaptized. In the typical edition, this permission applied to baptized, uncatechized Catholics, but the American edition has permitted validly baptized, uncatechized Christians of other denominations to participate in these as well.

The two Rites of Handing On the Creed and the Lord's Prayer formally present to the unbaptized two of the great pillars of Christian catechesis. Indeed, they form two of the four main divisions of the *Catechism of the Catholic Church* and have a long history of structuring the final preparation for those who will be baptized. Catechesis on the Creed schools them in the promises that they will make at their baptism, and catechesis on the Lord's Prayer prepares them to name God their Father once they become his adopted children at baptism.

Consequently, one should be cautious in offering these rites to those who are already baptized. Candidates are not preparing to make baptismal promises for the first time, and they are already numbered among the children of God. However, in cases of extreme lack of catechesis, or to help candidates baptized in a community that does not profess the Nicene Creed, some formation in these areas is essential, and the Rites of Handing On are permitted.

OCIA 407 says that they may be used in response to "the circumstance and spiritual benefit of these adults," and that they "signify God's action in this task of preparation." Still, for baptized candidates who have long professed the faith and called upon God the Father in prayer, it may seem disrespectful to ask them to undergo these rites.

A third rite is mentioned in 407, the Presentation of the Gospels. After the Second Vatican Council, the revisers of the catechumenate considered adding a third Rite of Handing On, a special liturgy in which the gospels were formally presented to the unbaptized.

Evidence for such a rite comes from the Gelasian Sacramentary of the mid-eighth century, and the revisers considered adopting a version of it. In the end, all that remains of it is in the Rite for Entrance into the Catechumenate. There, the celebrant helps the catechumens understand the dignity of God's word that they are about to hear (61), and later he may recite a formula when books containing the gospels are presented to the catechumens (64). This "Presentation of the Gospels" is what the American edition of OCIA 407 thinks the typical edition means.

However, the typical edition probably meant a completely distinct third Rite of Handing On, which the revisers at first inserted, later removed, and then overlooked this remaining shadow of their plans. The original Latin of 407 lists all three of these rites with the same title, showing their equivalency and independence. The Congregation for Divine Worship also assumed three separate Rites of Handing On in its 1973 Reflections, found in the appendix of this book. Nonetheless, the 2024 English translation in the United States calls the first two Rites of Handing On and the last a Rite of Presentation, which is what the 1988 translation also called the other two. If the presentation of the gospels is made, it takes place within the Rite of Welcoming (528).

The Handing On of the Creed is found among the rites for the unbaptized (157–63). Baptized candidates presumably celebrate it together with the unbaptized, though OCIA 407 does not state a preference. It could then happen during the third week of Lent with the elect, or at some other time of year during their formation (148, 157).

Liturgy of the Word

The recommended readings come from the Lectionary's ritual Masses. The presence of these readings in that volume signals a preference that this celebration take place at Mass. Indeed, OCIA 157 makes that clear. However, this is not to be done at one of the Sunday Masses, but on a weekday with the appropriate readings.

The first (Deut 6:1-7) presents a core teaching from the Bible. Moses begs the people of Israel to hear the words of the Lord, and to love the Lord their God with their whole heart. Embedded in this passage is belief in one God, who communicates with his people, and who expects them to respond with certain behavior. These same foundational beliefs underlie the Creed. They also review the stage of evangelization through which the unbaptized passed when they were inquirers. If they had no belief in God prior to their formation, now they do believe in monotheism. If some candidates had been baptized in infancy but never received religious formation or nurtured faith in God, this reading signals their new stage of development.

The responsorial draws from verses of Psalm 19, which praises the law of the Lord. For its refrain, the responsorial adopts a New Testament passage near the end of the sixth chapter of John's gospel. After Jesus delivered his discourse on the bread of life, some of those listening to him walked away, and Jesus wondered if his closest followers would do the same. Peter exclaimed that they had nowhere else to go because Jesus had the words of everlasting life. That simple statement of faith (John 6:68c) pairs with verses from Psalm 19 to sing the wonders of God's word and one's commitment to God's word. It frames that commitment with belief in Jesus Christ. The Creed is more than a state of beliefs. It is the central organizing principle of a Christian's life.

The Lectionary offers a choice for the second reading. In Romans 10:8-13, Paul summarizes the faith of those who believe in Christ, a faith that leads to salvation. These verses show the ultimate goal of the Creed. Paul makes a similar point in the alternate passage, 1 Corinthians 15:1-8a (or in the shorter version, verses 1-4). People will be saved if they hold fast to the Word of Christ, risen from the dead. That belief illuminates the fruitfulness of the Creed.

The verse accompanying the gospel acclamation is one of the most beloved by all Christians (John 3:16). It proclaims that God loved the world enough to send his Son so that he might bestow eternal life on all who believe. The Creed is much more than a list of catechetical points. It proclaims God's loving plan and offers a way of life in the present for those who hope for a salvation in the future.

Two options for the gospel complete the series of readings. The first recounts Peter's confession of faith and Jesus's promise to build his church upon that rock (Matt 16:13-18). In the alternate passage, Jesus proclaims that he entered the world as light so that those who believe in him might no longer dwell in darkness (John 12:44-50). All of these passages set up the formal bestowal of the Creed upon the elect and the uncatechized candidates.

Homily

The homily (159) may reflect on the purposes of Christian belief. As this preaching prepares the elect to receive the Creed, so it prepares the candidates to commit to its principles, which will direct their life.

Handing On of the Creed

The Handing On of the Creed may take place in one of two ways: The celebrant may recite it alone, or the community of the baptized may proclaim it to the elect and uncatechized candidates. As the OCIA and the Missal envision that this takes place at Mass, the presumed celebrant is a priest.

After the homily, the deacon or another minister invites the elect forward (160). The other minister could be a catechist or catechumenate coordinator if there is no deacon present. If uncatechized candidates are taking part, the invitation would need to change for them to come forward at this time. For example, he could say something like this:

> Let the elect and the candidates who still yearn for it come forward
> to receive from the church the Creed, the profession of faith.

The celebrant addresses the group, inviting them to listen to the Creed because of the mysteries it contains, to receive and to treasure it. His introduction presumes that these words are previously unfamiliar to those standing before him.

New to the revised translation is the option for the celebrant to proclaim the Creed alone. This option has always existed in the typical edition, but it was not included in the 1988 English edition. In support of this option, when the celebrant speaks the Creed alone, he takes on his presidential role, personally handing on the Creed to those who are to receive it among this new generation of Christians.

However, the celebrant may begin the Creed, declaring his own faith, and the faithful may take up the rest of it together with him. In this version, validly baptized, catechized candidates could number themselves among the faithful and join in handing on the Creed to the others.

Prayer over the Elect

The celebrant invites people to join him in a prayer over the elect (161). They will pray that the God of mercy will forgive the sins of the elect through their baptism.

The OCIA does not offer alternative wording for this prayer, but because it invites candidates to take part in the rite, and because it permits the usage of similar words to those provided, the celebrant could invite the community to pray not only for the elect, but also for any uncatechized candidates in the group. For example, he could add these words to the given introduction:

> Let us also pray for these candidates,
> that receiving remission of all their sins through the sacrament of penance,
> they too may be strengthened in Christ Jesus our Lord.

The prayer, similarly, presumes that all those who have just received the Creed are not yet baptized. The celebrant would have to adjust the words that ask God to make these individuals worthy of attaining not only the grace of baptism but also reception into the full communion of the church. For example, after reciting the prayer for the elect, the celebrant could add words such as these:

> Look also upon these candidates N. and N.,
> and make them worthy of receiving the Body and Blood of Christ.

Dismissal of the Elect

The elect may be dismissed (162). The minister who gives the dismissal and the options for dismissing and remaining are the same as those explained above in the Rite for Entrance and its combination with the Rite of Welcoming (528).

Here, because the candidates have been baptized, they are not among those to be dismissed at any stage. Their baptism gives them a place praying with others in the community as the Mass continues.

Permission for baptized, uncatechized adults to take part in this ritual creates some challenges for maintaining its integrity. Nonetheless, the OCIA permits uncatechized candidates to join the elect in receiving the Creed.

Handing On of the Lord's Prayer

The traditional occasion for handing on the Lord's Prayer is a weekday Mass in the fifth week of Lent (178). Surely, it would be rare for a validly baptized Christian not to have learned the Lord's Prayer by this point of their formation, but the OCIA permits such adults to join the elect in receiving this important prayer.

For the unbaptized, the rite may be conducted at another time of year, even during the period of the catechumenate before the Rite of Election, or later, during the Preparation Rites on Holy Saturday (149, 178). For the baptized, the rite could take place at any time of their formation, as their reception is not linked to the liturgical year.

Liturgy of the Word

The readings are found in the *Lectionary for Mass*, signaling again the assumption that this ceremony takes place at Mass and that the presider is therefore a priest. The first reading (Hos 11:1b, 3-4, 8e-9) paints a picture of God as a loving parent holding a child with love and withholding wrathful punishment. This is the God whom Jesus permitted his followers to call their Father—just as he did.

For the responsorial the Lectionary offers two choices. Psalm 23 is the classic popular prayer declaring the Lord as one's shepherd. Psalm 103 chooses as its refrain the belief that the Lord's compassion on those who fear him is like that of a father for his children. Both of these Old Testament passages take on a Christian hue in the context of this celebration. Through baptism, Christians call God their Father.

The second reading also offers a choice. In both instances (Rom 8:14-17, 26-27; Gal 4:4-7), Paul encourages his readers to call God "Abba," a familial, intimate title for their Father. As Jesus is the incarnate Son of God, so all the followers of Jesus are adopted children of God. Jesus and his followers all use this affectionate term for the First Person of the Trinity: "Father."

The versicle for the gospel acclamation draws from the first of these options for the second reading (Rom 8:15). Paul declares that the Romans did not receive a spirit of slavery, but a spirit of adoption. This permits them to call upon God as their Father.

The gospel is the Lord's Prayer, and even when a deacon assists at this Mass, even if there are concelebrants, the priest celebrant proclaims it because he is the one handing on the prayer to the group. The deacon invites the elect and any uncatechized candidates forward. When the bishop presides, he rises from his place before proclaiming the gospel, suggesting that the elect (and candidates) are to come stand around the cathedra. From there he proclaims the sacred text (*Ceremonial of Bishops* 422). Presumably, a priest celebrant also remains at the presider's chair to proclaim this gospel.

First the celebrant addresses the group, inviting them to listen to the words that Jesus taught. He then proclaims the Lord's Prayer and concludes with "The Gospel of the Lord" (180).

In this dramatic, intimate handing on of the gospel, it is Christ who teaches the Lord's Prayer to his disciples once again. All hear the celebrant's voice, but it is Christ who speaks and teaches his disciples how to pray.

Homily

A homily follows (181). This explains the meaning and importance of the prayer that the group has just heard.

Prayer over the Elect

The celebrant then asks the faithful present to join him in prayer (182). The invitation references the elect who are approaching the waters of baptism. This is exactly the introduction he gave at the Handing On of the Creed (161). The celebrant may therefore add on these or similar words, as indicated above:

> Let us also pray for these candidates,
> that receiving remission of all their sins through the sacrament
> of penance,
> they too may be strengthened in Christ Jesus our Lord.

The prayer that follows also refers to the upcoming baptism. The celebrant will need to add some words of the prayer for those who have already been reborn in the font of baptism and were already numbered among the adopted children. For example, he could add an invocation such as this:

> Increase also the faith and understanding of these candidates,
> and welcome them to your holy table.
> Through Christ our Lord.

The dismissal follows, as in the Rite of Handing On the Creed (183). Regarding the minister who gives the dismissal and the formulas he may use, the same options from the previous rites reappear (162, 528). If the service continues with the Liturgy of the Eucharist, as it should, then the candidates would remain.

The participation of validly baptized Christians in these two rituals is awkward because of their purpose, words, and ritual elements. The OCIA had in mind the possible participation of baptized, uncatechized *Catholics* in this ritual. However, even that restriction would have opened similar questions: Why is a baptized person being treated like those who have not been baptized? Why invite them to participate in services at which the prayers make no concession to the baptism that they experienced? How could one presume that baptized candidates should not already be calling upon God as their Father, or that their praying of the Lord's Prayer at the next celebration of the Mass would carry special significance, as it does for neophytes (149)?

These two rituals are not necessary for candidates, and they are not appropriate for candidates who have already received fundamental catechesis. It is more expressive if only the unbaptized receive the Creed and the Lord's Prayer.

Rite of Sending the Candidates for the Calling to Continuing Conversion

The Meaning

The Rite of Sending and the Rite for Calling form a pair. The first, the Rite of Sending, may take place in the parish. It leads toward the second, usually celebrated at the cathedral, where, in many dioceses, the combined Rites of Election and for Calling the Candidates to Continuing Conversion take place. The cathedral forms an impressive backdrop for these ceremonies and instills a broader sense of identity in the diocesan church.

Given the number of participants, and due to limited space at the cathedral, many people in the home parishes are therefore unable to celebrate this step with the candidates preparing to join the church. In the United States, the Rite of Sending was created for the parishes. It first appeared in the 1988 translation. It invites local testimony about the progress of the candidates and secures the prayers of the parish community.

The two types of candidates are distinguished: Catholics completing their sacraments of initiation and other Christians to be received (434). All may celebrate this rite recognizing a stage in their formation.

This rite is modeled after the Rite of Sending Catechumens for Election (106–17). It too was created for use in the United States, and it also first appeared in 1988. There is no Latin original for either Rite of Sending in the Vatican's typical edition. The Rite of Sending Catechumens, in turn, is modeled after the Rite of Election or Enrollment of Names (118–37), a pivotal turning point in the process for the unbaptized in which they are more formally enrolled among the elect, those chosen for the rites of initiation. They are still catechumens, but their title changes to "elect." No such change in title accompanies the candidates who complete these adapted rites.

The inspiration for the Rite of Sending probably comes from OCIA 130, where, at the presentation of the catechumens in the Rite of Election, an accommodation is made for a celebration with a large number of them. They may be presented as a group by their own catechist. "But in this case, the catechists should be advised to call each catechumen forward by name in a special celebration held before they come to the common rite."

In the United States, the Rite of Election is commonly held at the cathedral or another large church and gathers large numbers from parishes across the diocese. Therefore, the English edition offers a complete preliminary rite in which catechists may call each catechumen by name in their home parish. OCIA 130 highlights this as an occasion for calling, not for sending, but the US edition frames this adapted rite as one in which the local community not only names the catechumens but sends them to the cathedral.

At many diocesan celebrations of the Rite of Election, the names of the catechumens are read out, even if they were read at the preliminary celebration in the parish. The sending therefore constitutes more of a goodwill gesture that allows more people in the parish to partner with the catechumens at this pivotal stage by hearing their names, praying for their progress, and sending them forth.

Usually a liturgical sending is a dismissal from the assembly of believers and into the world. This sending is unique in that it sends a subgroup from one liturgy into another, and from one church to another.

The OCIA in the United States supplies a Rite of Sending for uncatechized candidates to the combined Rites of Election and for Calling, usually at the cathedral. The candidates too may be called by name in a special celebration at the local parish prior to the diocesan observance.

The Title

The revised English translation has changed the title of this rite. The 1988 edition called it the Rite of Sending the Candidates for Recognition by the Bishop and for the Call to Continuing Conversion. The words "for Recognition by the Bishop" have been removed.

The opening paragraphs still speak about the candidates' recognition by the bishop and defend it based on the unity that the bishop represents (435). When conversing about this rite, many people call it the occasion when the candidates go to the cathedral to meet the bishop. However, its purpose is to call its participants to continuing conversion. The removal of the words from the title diminishes the unintended promotion of the bishop's celebrity status and underscores the spiritual journey of the candidates, the proper focus of this rite.

The removal of the words created a discrepancy in the use of a preposition in the titles of the first and second of these rites. The heading for the first one at OCIA 434 says that the Rite of Sending is "for" the Calling to Continuing Conversion. The heading for the second at OCIA 446 is entitled the Rite "of" Calling to Continuing Conversion. Furthermore, the 1988 English edition used "Call to Conversion" in the Rite of Sending but "Calling to Conversion" in the subsequent rite. Now both refer to the "Calling" to Conversion. A more complete title above OCIA 434 would have been "Rite of Sending the Candidates for the Rite of the Calling to Continuing Conversion," but that is a mouthful.

The Location

The cathedral itself symbolizes diocesan unity, and many of those involved in Christian initiation in the United States presume that it is the preferred location for the Rite of Election of the catechumens—and therefore the preferred location for the Rite of Calling to Continuing Conversion for the candidates. Worth noting, though, is that the typical edition in Latin simply says that the Rite of Election should take place "in a church or, if necessary, in a suitable and fitting place," permitting a celebration outside a church altogether. The recommendation that the Rite of Election take place at the cathedral appears only in the English edition in the United States (127). One wonders if the typical edition implied that bishops could delegate pastors to conduct the complete rite in their parish churches.

Celebrating the Rite of Election at the cathedral has borne great fruit. Participants experience the scope of the local church, the personal ministry of their bishop, and the blossoming activity of the Holy Spirit at work in the hearts of those seeking to follow God's call. In some dioceses the cathedral is so small that the celebrations take place at another church or are repeated in order to accommodate the number of participants.

Candidates are not required to go to the cathedral for the Rite of Calling. That rite may take place in the parish church (448). The explanation that opens this rite calls it optional (434). The 1988 English translation stated that it prepares for a subsequent celebration, "for example, at the cathedral with the bishop." That example has been removed from OCIA 434. If the Rite of Calling takes place in the parish and not at the cathedral, there is no point in celebrating the Rite of Sending. The candidates are not being sent anywhere. The parallel rite for catechumens in the United States explicitly makes that point (106).

The Combined Rite

OCIA 436 situates the Rite of Sending at the parish community, and 437 shows where to find the version of this rite combined with the parallel one for catechumens. The revised translation again removes the word "recognition" from both of these numbers, appropriately separating the person of the bishop from the meaning of the rite.

In the combined rite, these explanatory paragraphs are essentially the same as those in the 1988 English edition (530–35). However, OCIA 530 removes the location of the subsequent celebration, "for example, at the cathedral with the bishop," and instead notes that the theological and liturgical introduction for the parallel rite for catechumens will supply more information, citing 106–9. In what is surely an oversight, the 2024 English edition has retained being "presented to the Bishop" as one purpose of the combined rite (532).

Although many people have derived benefit from having validly baptized candidates participate in the combined Rites of Sending to Election and Calling at the cathedral, this was never part of the original vision for the reception of candidates. After the necessary formation, they were to be received into the full communion of the church without intervening steps.

Those who developed the 1972 Order of Reception for validly baptized candidates probably would have viewed the Rite of Sending and the Rite for Calling, as well as the involvement of a bishop and a cathedral, as unnecessary detours to the sharing of communion. To restate an important point, these adapted rites are only for those candidates who have had very little Christian formation. Others omit these steps and are received into the church at any time of year as they are ready.

Liturgy of the Word: Homily

In the Liturgy of the Word, the celebrant offers a homily addressed not only to the candidates, but to everyone (438). All are to be good examples and accompany the candidates on their path. The instructions for this homily are based on those for the Rite of Election of the unbaptized (129). In the combined rite, the description of the homily evokes "the path of the Paschal Mystery" (536), an expression that comes from the description of the homily for catechumens. It is less relevant for candidates who have already been baptized.

In practice, if the Rite of Sending takes place at a parish Sunday Mass, the celebrant may give the homily he has prepared for other Masses that weekend. The homily is not the only time during Mass when the celebrant may encourage the gathered faithful to care for the candidates.

Presentation of the Candidates

The Presentation of the Candidates follows (439). In the combined rite, the entire Presentation of the Catechumens (537–39), copied from 111–13, precedes the Presentation of the Candidates (540–42), copied from 439–41.

The person responsible for the formation of the candidates, or some other representative from the community, introduces the rite by addressing the celebrant. The speaker testifies that the candidates have made spiritual progress, have received the community's support, and now ask for recognition of their status.

This is largely the same introduction from the 1988 edition, now printed in sense lines for the convenience of the speaker. However, in that edition the catechist or representative explained to the celebrant that the candidates were going to be recognized by the local bishop, and even mentioned him by name. That explanation has been removed in a provident attempt to keep the purpose of the rite focused on continuing conversion, not on the prominence of the bishop.

This introduction presumes that the rite at the cathedral is taking place later the same day, or on a subsequent Sunday or other day. Dioceses exercise some freedom on scheduling the Rite of Election, even though the OCIA recommends it for the First Sunday of Lent (128). The Roman Missal's Ritual Mass for the Election or Enrollment of Names also presumes it takes place on the First Sunday of Lent, though it permits a different day.

The celebrant invites the candidates and sponsors forward. This parallels the Rite of Sending the Catechumens (111) and the Rite of Election (130). The revised English edition has changed the persons whom the celebrant addresses from "those who are to be recognized" to "candidates" (439). This subtle change keeps the purpose of the ritual in check—not a recognition by the bishop but an internal call to spiritual renewal. It also preserves a consistent use of the word "candidates."

One by one, the candidates are called by name (439). The speaker is not identified, but it would appropriately be the same catechist or representative who presented them. The Rite of Election offers the option of presenting small groups of catechumens without calling their names, but the adapted Rites of Sending call for each name to be announced. This fulfills the expectation of OCIA 130, ensuring that the individual names be read aloud at some point of this stage. Especially for the catechumen, the personal calling by name fits their discernment that Christ calls them to the waters of new life.

The candidates are to stand before the celebrant (439). Each church sanctuary is unique, so the arranging of the candidates may vary from one parish to another. They are best positioned where they may have direct eye contact with the celebrant, are seen by others in the assembly, yet do not block their view. It may prove beneficial in some sanctuaries for the celebrant to stand between the candidates and the assembly, so that he can more naturally turn to each group of people as he addresses them, and the assembly can see the faces of the candidates.

Affirmation by the Sponsors (and the Assembly)

The celebrant secures the affirmation of the sponsors and the assembly (440). The suggested words are based on a similar address from the Rite of Election (131A). The sample from the 1988 English edition is repeated here without revision, though now in sense lines to assist the proclamation. The parallels between the two addresses would have been easier to grasp if these words had been revised as well.

Significantly, the celebrant of the Rite of Election acknowledges that the catechumens have tried to live according to the commands of Christ, but in this address the celebrant of the Rite of Sending the Candidates says that they have tried to follow the commands of Christ "more perfectly." This acknowledges that they were doing so in some measure in the past because of their baptism.

The revised translation of 131A makes a stronger allusion to Acts of the Apostles 2:42, which describes the first Christians sharing in communion and prayer. The 2024 English edition does not take advantage of that stronger allusion in the celebrant's address concerning the candidates (440).

The celebrant then announces that the community ratifies the decision of the candidates (440). This is based on OCIA 131A, where, at the Rite of Election, the celebrant is presumed to have been part of the deliberation and is bringing forth the discernment of the leadership. In this Rite of Sending, both as the presider and a member of the community, the celebrant is presumed to have had previous participation in the deliberation concerning the candidates' progress.

The celebrant asks the sponsors to restate their opinion in public (440). His words acknowledge the potential existence of both groups of candidates: baptized, uncatechized Catholics seeking the sacraments of confirmation and Communion, and other uncatechized Christians seeking reception.

When making his address to the community, the celebrant of the Rite of Sending may use similar words to those provided (440). Taking all of the above into consideration, he could say something like this:

> My dear brothers and sisters,
> these candidates, already one with us by reason of their baptism in Christ,
> have asked to complete their initiation
> (or: have asked to be received into the full communion of the Catholic Church).
> Those who know them have judged
> that they are sincere in their desire.
> For some time they have listened to Christ's word
> and have tried to live according to his commands more perfectly;
> they have shared in fraternal communion and in the prayers.
> Now I make known to the whole congregation
> that our community ratifies their desire
> to complete their initiation
> (or: to be received into full communion).
> Therefore, I ask their sponsors to give their recommendation again, in your presence.
> With God as your witness, do you judge these candidates

> ready to receive the sacraments of confirmation and the Eucharist
> (or: ready to be received into the full communion of the Catholic Church)?

The celebrant may ask the entire congregation for its affirmation (440). This too is inspired by a similar option in the Rite of Election for catechumens (131A). However, the 2024 English edition, like its predecessor, does not offer a scripted question. It simply permits the celebrant to say something. A question based on 131A could be this:

> Now I ask you, the members of this community: Are you willing to affirm the testimony expressed about these candidates and include them in your prayer and affection?

The celebrant finally addresses the candidates and sends them to the Calling to Continuing Conversion (441). Some words from the 1988 edition have been revised. For example, "sends you to Bishop N." has become "sends you to the Calling to Continuing Conversion, where Bishop N. will exhort you." The celebrant sends the candidates to a specific ceremony, not generically to a bishop.

As in the 1988 edition, the candidates have said nothing throughout this rite. Their sponsors have spoken on their behalf, and the whole congregation may have done so as well. Based on this testimony and their mere presence, they are sent forth.

Universal Prayer (Prayer of the Faithful)

The universal prayer follows. As in the 1988 edition, the revision provides no scripted introduction for the celebrant (442). Many priests daily improvise their own introduction to the universal prayer, and the rite seems to presume that the celebrant will do the same here.

The combined rite offers an introduction (543). It comes from the rite pertaining to the catechumens (114), though it adds a reference to the candidates. Because of the catechumens, this combined rite more fittingly takes place at the beginning of Lent, as the introduction presumes.

In the uncombined Rite of Sending the Candidates, the celebrant could introduce the universal prayer with words that avoid references to Lent and Easter, such as the following:

> Dear brothers and sisters,
> these candidates, who look forward to
> (reception into the full communion of the church and)
> a sharing the sacraments of confirmation and Communion
> look to us for an example of faithfulness to the church.
> Therefore, let us pray to the Lord for them and for ourselves,
> that being encouraged by our mutual faith,
> we may be made worthy of the grace of God.

However, the Rite of Sending the Candidates would likely not be celebrated at another time of year. The candidates may celebrate the Rite of Calling to Continuing Conversion at the parish church, which would eliminate the need for sending them somewhere else. Or both of these Rites (Sending and Calling) may be omitted.

OCIA 442 offers several sample petitions, of which one or more may be included with the other petitions for the church and the world. As in the Rite of Welcoming, a "lector" is to read these. However, that person need not be a lector whom the bishop has instituted; an ordinary reader or a deacon may read the petitions.

These intentions are based on the revised translation of the ones in the Rite of Sending the Catechumens (114), which in turn have collected and rearranged its petitions from the Rite of Election (134A and B). The only difference is that the petition for godparents prays also for the sponsors. The rearrangement matches those from the 1988 English edition. The final petition mentions the current or coming Lenten season, assuming that the candidates are going to be received at the Easter Vigil, which may not be the case. Another option for this petition is to remove that reference altogether, like this:

> For our community, that it may be radiant
> with the fullness of charity and with constancy in prayer,
> let us pray to the Lord.

Nonetheless, it would be rare to celebrate this rite apart from this time of year. As noted above, if the candidates are celebrating the Calling to Continuing Conversion at the parish, there is no Rite of Sending. A calling to conversion makes sense during Lent; it is harder to explain at other times of the year.

The combined rite repeats the petitions from the Rite of Sending the Candidates (543, see 442), adding catechumens to the first petition. Those planning to celebrate the combined rite could remove and replace some of these or compose a completely new set of petitions.

In the uncombined Rite of Sending the Candidates, the celebrant extends his hands over them and concludes the petitions with a prayer (443). The source for this prayer is the second option at the Rite of Election (135B), which specifically prays for the elect. That word changes to "catechumens" in the Rite of Sending the Catechumens (115), and to "candidates" in the Rite of Sending the Candidates (443). The combined Rite of Sending changes it to "catechumens and candidates" (544). Otherwise, it is the same prayer. In all these versions the celebrant extends his hands over the pertinent group.

Dismissal of the Assembly or Celebration of the Eucharist

The rite may conclude at this point with a dismissal of the entire assembly (444). Alternatively, the Liturgy of the Eucharist may follow (445). There is no option for dismissing the candidates while the rest of the community remains. If Mass continues, all of those already baptized may join in the upcoming prayers.

The 1988 English edition assigned the dismissal to the celebrant. In the revised, the person who gives the dismissal is unnamed. If a priest has been assisted by a deacon, the deacon would appropriately give the dismissal.

As in other instances of this formula (432, for example), the second English edition removes the word "always" that had been added to the 1988 edition. It had never been part of the dismissals of the typical edition, and it must have seemed an unnecessary addition.

The combined rite includes the options for dismissing the catechumens when the Liturgy of the Eucharist follows (545, see 116). The uncombined Rite of Sending the Candidates does not mention a dismissal of catechumens (444), but if this rite takes place when catechumens not preparing for their immediate initiation are present, that group, who still await a date for their Rite of Election, may be dismissed.

The heading "Celebration of the Eucharist" reappears in 445 as in 433. "Liturgy of the Eucharist" would have been more accurate.

In the combined rite, OCIA 546 says that the Eucharist is celebrated after the dismissal. This accounts for the dismissal of catechumens before the universal prayer, while copying the instructions from the Rite of Sending the Catechumens (117).

The Creed is recited on Sundays and solemnities. If this rite takes place during a Mass that normally requires the Creed, whether uncombined or combined with the Rite of Sending Catechumens, the Creed may be omitted for unspecified "pastoral reasons" (445, 546). This probably accommodates the length of the ceremony on a Sunday when many Americans fret at Masses that may extend over an hour. The permission is unfortunate in that the Creed contains the beliefs shared by the faithful with the candidates. The same permission appears in the Rite of Election and in the scrutinies.

Rite of Calling the Candidates to Continuing Conversion

Those Who Qualify

The candidates who may celebrate this rite are either uncatechized Catholic adults preparing for confirmation and Communion or other Christians preparing for reception (446). Again, the two groups of baptized candidates are named—Catholics and those from other Christian denominations.

When describing the adults who qualify for this rite, the second English edition removes the word "previously" before "uncatechized" for clarity. These optional rites are for those who did not receive catechesis. Baptized Catholic adults who have received their First Communion and are in formation for confirmation are not to be included in this rite. They presumably received catechesis in preparation for their First Communion.

This rite may be combined with the Rite of Election. In that case, OCIA 547 invites in addition to the catechumens any "candidates preparing either for Confirmation, Eucharist or Reception." This could be construed to mean that adult candidates for confirmation may be included. However, OCIA 400 and 446 make it clear that only Catholic adults lacking formation and celebration of both confirmation and Communion participate.

The uncombined Rite of Calling is designed for communities that have candidates but no catechumens (447). It may even be used in parishes with catechumens, but whose candidates are preparing for reception at a different time of year than Lent. When the entire group in formation has already been baptized, they may celebrate this rite with their pastor in their parish church (448).

For more background, the combined rite directs people to study the theological and liturgical introduction on these ceremonies (547). These are found at OCIA 118–27 and 446–49.

Occasion and Presider

The Rite of Calling may be celebrated at the beginning of Lent with the bishop or pastor presiding (448). This short paragraph underwent several revisions. Instead of declaring that the rite "is" celebrated at the beginning of Lent, the words clarify that it "may be" celebrated at that time. Uncatechized candidates could undergo this ceremony at other times of year.

The recommendation for celebrating this rite at the start of Lent comes from OCIA 409, now properly noted in 448. The suggestion comes from a paragraph that treats baptized but uncatechized adult Catholics. The original Latin typical edition suggested having those Catholics celebrate the sacraments of confirmation and Communion at the Easter Vigil. Again, the original edition never recommended receiving those baptized in other denominations into the full communion of the church at the Easter Vigil. The English translation permits it and explains how to do it.

Furthermore, the designation of the presider has now been expanded from the pastor of the parish to "the Bishop or the pastor of the parish." In many dioceses, this rite is observed in its combined form with the bishop presiding over the ceremony. Rarely would the bishop preside over this particular rite without catechumens, but OCIA 448 indicates that it may be done that way.

For the combined rite, the bishop or his delegate presides, presumably at the cathedral, normally on the First Sunday of Lent (548), even though those baptized in other denominations may experience this liturgy at another time of year. This description of the combined rite has led to a widespread practice of bishops celebrating it in their cathedral at the beginning of Lent for both catechumens and candidates.

Liturgy of the Word

The Rite of Calling the Candidates takes place during the Liturgy of the Word after the homily. The celebrant of this uncombined rite, usually the pastor, is to give the homily addressing the candidates and the entire community who accompany them in their final preparation for confirmation and Communion (450). When this rite is combined with the Rite of Election, the bishop or his presiding delegate gives the homily (550).

The description of the homily in the uncombined rite is adapted from the one for the parallel Rite of Election (129). That homily notes that the elect are embarking on the path of the paschal mystery, which includes their baptism. This homily may focus on the other sacraments. The *reception* of baptized Christians from other denominations is not mentioned in 450 but may be inferred.

Celebration of Election: Presentation of the Catechumens

In the combined rite, the person responsible for the initiation of the catechumens presents them first, before the baptized candidates (551). This inspired the similar sequence in the Rite of Sending the Catechumens (111). At a diocesan celebration, the person who presents the group is often a deacon. However, another diocesan representative of formation may introduce the entire group.

The celebrant invites those chosen to come forward with their godparents. The names of the catechumens are called out one by one (551). Often someone from each parish who knows how to pronounce the names reads the local list. Alternatively, someone may simply announce the name of the parish, but in that case the names of those seeking baptism must have been read aloud beforehand in a special celebration, such as the Rite of Sending.

Celebration of Election: Affirmation by the Godparents (and the Assembly)

The godparents give testimony about the catechumens (552). This testimony repeats at the cathedral the testimony that may have been given in the Rite of Sending at the parish (112). If the bishop is presiding at the Rite of Election, it is unlikely that he has taken part in the deliberation about the readiness of the catechumens, so he most likely uses option B or similar words. If he has been part of the deliberation, he may use either option A or B.

In either case, after completing this step, he has yet another option: He may ask the entire assembly to affirm the testimony and to include the catechumens in their prayer and affection. If so, all declare that they are ready for that responsibility. It is hard to imagine why the bishop would omit this request of the assembly, but he may. The typical edition in Latin permitted such a question but did not supply one. The edition for the United States helpfully includes a formula, which stands as the basis for the one adapted for the candidates.

The entire Rite of Election hinges on the testimony of the godparents. The celebrant's declaration that these catechumens are numbered among the elect relies on their voice. Consequently, it is essential that the godparents be present for this liturgy.

Celebration of Election: Questioning and Petitioning of the Catechumens

The celebrant questions the catechumens about their intentions and invites them to offer their names for enrollment (553). In some cases, they may have already inscribed their names in a preceding parish celebration (113).

For the enrollment, the catechumens may inscribe their own names, or they may call out their names for the godparents or the one who presented them to create the list in the Book of the Elect (119). This action gives the ritual its alternative title, the Rite of Enrollment of Names. In Latin, the title is in the singular: The Rite of Enrollment of [One's] Name. Each name is significant—not just the collection of names.

In the United States, if the number of catechumens is large, and if they have already signed their names in a parish Book of the Elect during the Rite of Sending (113), that book may be presented to the bishop during the diocesan Rite of Election. A spokesperson may tell the bishop the name of the parish from which the names come. As the document is presented, the bishop receives the list of names.

The Rite of Election allows contrasting options: The names may be announced aloud twice, once, or not be announced at all. In the presentation of the catechumens, their names may be read a first time, and at their inscription their names may be announced to the person who enrolls their names. Or one of these announcements may be omitted. Or, if their names had been announced at a parish celebration, they may be presented as a group, and then individually write their own names in the book without anyone announcing them aloud.

During the enrollment, a suitable chant may be sung, and OCIA 553 recommends Psalm 16. Its verses declare how the individual chooses the Lord and not other gods. They also declare confidence that God will not abandon them to the netherworld but show them the path of life. Even as the catechumens are enrolling their names among the elect, the community may sing of one's devout choice to remain within the refuge of God.

The bishop declares these catechumens to be among the elect, those chosen for initiation at the upcoming Easter Vigil. He invites the godparents to indicate their intent to care for them (554). For example, they may place a hand on the shoulder of the elect or embrace them. This concludes the Rite of Election proper.

Celebration of the Calling to Continuing Conversion: Presentation of the Candidates for Confirmation and the Eucharist

In the combined rite, the Calling to Continuing Conversion for the candidates follows. The ritual happens in the same way that it may take place uncombined at a parish (OCIA 555–57, see 451–54).

The rite for candidates alone begins with the Presentation of the Candidates for Confirmation and the Eucharist (451). This imitates the Presentation of the Catechumens in the Rite of Election (130).

Although the title suggests that the rite pertains only to uncatechized Catholics, it includes the candidates for reception. The combined rite more appropriately simplifies the title to Presentation of the Candidates (555), which includes adult Catholics and leaves open the possible presence of candidates from other denominations who also need reception. As noted above, it would be highly inappropriate to include candidates from Eastern Orthodoxy in this ritual, who only require a simple profession of faith (474). The discrepancy in the titles has been carried over from the 1988 edition.

The person responsible for the formation of the candidates presents them to the celebrant (451). The suggested formula is based on the one from the Rite of Election (130). The 1988 English edition made optional an expression about the approach of Easter because this ceremony could take place at another time of year. However, the same edition in the same paragraph referred to "this Lenten season," which presumed that Easter was drawing near after all. The 2024 English edition has fittingly removed the reference to Lent and changed this second expression to "due preparation." The combined rite copies the same revised wording (555).

The presentation refers to both kinds of candidates—Catholics and other Christians. It concludes with an unfortunately imprecise expression about the second group. The 1988 English edition called them those asking for admission "to full eucharistic sharing." This has changed to "full Eucharistic Communion" (451). However, they are asking for reception into the full communion of the Catholic Church, which will then immediately lead to the sacraments of confirmation and Holy Communion. The candidates are seeking full ecclesial communion, which will lead to Eucharistic Communion.

The celebrant invites the candidates forward with their sponsors (451 and 555). This too is based on the invitation from the Rite of Election. The celebrant calls the candidates "those who desire to participate fully in the sacramental life of the Church," which is a good description of their status. However, for those baptized in other denominations, their desire is not just sacramental; it is ecclesial. They are asking for the fullness of the church, not just the fullness of the sacraments.

The individual candidates are called by name, presumably by the person who presents them to the celebrant. Each approaches the celebrant with the sponsor who accompanies them (451). In the combined rite, if there are a great many candidates, they are presented in groups—not by name—by the catechists responsible for them. OCIA 555 does not indicate what they are to say, but judging from OCIA 553, they probably give the name of the parish. For example, each representative making the presentation could say something like one of these options:

> These are the names of the candidates for Reception into the Full Communion of the Catholic Church and for the sacraments of confirmation and Communion.

> Here present are the candidates from the parish of N. seeking reception into the full communion of the Catholic Church and the sacraments of confirmation and Communion.

In the second case, some other ceremony should be held in which the candidates are called by name. OCIA 555 gives no other information about the structure of such a ceremony, but the Rite of Sending would fulfill this need.

The names of the candidates do not bear the same ritual weight as the names of the catechumens. The catechumens are being numbered individually among the elect, those chosen for baptism. The candidates are already baptized, and their names have long identified them as bearers of that status. The Calling to Continuing Conversion was created for the United States, where it offers ritual attention to the candidates. Calling out the candidates' names seems at least a courteous thing to do for those who have undergone a period of discernment and formation similar to the unbaptized. However, the decision to make the calling of their names imitate the calling of names of the unbaptized may cloud the significance of the specific names being enrolled for baptism. The Calling to Continuing Conversion is optional, but the Rite of Election is essential.

Celebration of the Calling to Continuing Conversion: Affirmation by the Sponsors (and the Assembly)

The celebrant addresses all those in attendance with an instruction adapted from the Rite of Election (452 and 556, see 131). He may use words similar to two options presented in the book, depending on whether or not he was personally involved with the deliberation, as is the case with the bishop in the Rite of Election.

An address similar to the first option has already appeared in the Rite of Sending (440A); however, the revised English edition adjusted those words to align more closely with the ones from the Rite of Election. The same edition overlooks those changes and basically re-presents the address from the 1988 edition (452A and 556A).

This address again refers to the candidates as those who ask "to participate fully in the sacramental life of the Catholic Church." However, those validly baptized in other denominations are asking admission into the full communion of the church in order to receive the sacraments. Additionally, uncatechized, baptized Catholic candidates already enjoy the full communion of the Catholic Church. Only one line has been updated for the revised edition, the one alluding to the first Christians in Acts of the Apostles: "They have shared in fraternal communion and in the prayers."

The address concludes with revised instructions pertaining to the sponsors. The 1988 edition had the celebrant say, "I ask their sponsors now to state their opinion once again, so that all of you may hear." The 2024 edition takes more inspiration from its revised words in the Rite of Election: "As I inform you of this judgment and speak to the sponsors, I ask them to give their recommendation again, in your presence." The Rite of Sending still uses the same language from the 1988 edition (440A).

A version of this address appears in the Rite of Sending the Catechumens, the Rite of Election, the Rite of Sending the Candidates, the Calling to Continuing Conversion, and the combined versions of these rites. It is not surprising that the editors overlooked updates in one section when preparing another.

The celebrant addresses the sponsors (452A and 556A). Using a question based on the one from the Rite of Election (131A), he asks if they judge the candidates worthy of the sacraments or of reception. They give their assent.

The celebrant may ask the entire congregation for its support in faith, prayer, and example (453 and 556A). This too is based on a similar question from the Rite of Election (131A). That question was supplied for the 1988 edition in the United States because the typical edition permits a question at the Rite of Election but does not supply one.

A second option to ascertain the affirmation of the sponsors questions them directly. The celebrant asks their judgment on individual areas of the candidates' formation (453 and 552B).

The first question copies one from the Rite of Election (131B). In the 1988 edition, the celebrant asked sponsors if the candidates had listened to "the apostles' instruction," an allusion to Acts 2:42. Now he asks if they listened to "God's word," which is the expression from the Rite of Election and expands the inquiry to embrace the entire Bible, not just the New Testament.

The remaining questions are unique to the Rite of Calling and are more specific to the experience of baptized candidates. They ask about a deeper appreciation of baptism, reflection on the tradition of the church, and joining other baptized brothers and sisters in prayer. These are taken exactly from the 1988 edition for which they were composed.

One question aimed to imitate the final question in the Rite of Election, "Have they persevered in fraternal communion and in the prayers," which, as noted above, also alluded to Acts 2:42. The allusion remains, asking if they have "joined their brothers and sisters in prayer." But this question in OCIA 453B of the revised edition did not take advantage of the revised translation of the parallel question in OCIA 131B. The celebrant, who may use similar words, could ask something like this:

> Have they reflected sufficiently on the tradition of the church,
> which is their heritage, and persevered in fraternal
> communion and in the prayers?

The list of questions concludes with another one unique to the candidates, inquiring if they have advanced in love and service to others. This was taken from the 1988 edition and remains an appropriate point of inquiry.

Sponsors are to answer these questions honestly. They rely on their own experience with the candidates, as well as the testimony of the catechists and other representatives of the community.

The optional question to the assembly is lifted from the 1988 edition. It is identical to the one from the Rite of Election except for exchanging the word "catechumens" with "candidates" and putting the words "as we move toward Easter" in parentheses, which acknowledges the option of celebrating this rite at any time of year.

Celebration of the Calling to Continuing Conversion: Act of Recognition

The rite for candidates moves immediately to its Act of Recognition (454 and 557). In the Rite of Election, the celebrant asks the catechumens if it is their will to receive the sacraments of Christian initiation. They give their assent and are invited to sign the Book of the Elect (132 and 553). In this case, the candidates are not asked to declare their intention, which, for the catechumens, pertains more to baptism than to the other sacraments. Nor do the candidates offer their names for enrollment, which is a prebaptismal act. Instead, the celebrant recognizes their assumed desire and asks them to "hear the Lord's call to continuing conversion," while remaining faithful to their baptismal covenant. The candidates respond, "Thanks be to God" (454 and 557).

The celebrant asks the sponsors to continue supporting the candidates with their guidance and concern. His admonitions to the candidates and the sponsors are directly taken from the 1988 edition, for which they were composed. The only difference is that the reference to "this Lent" in the uncombined rite appears in parentheses in case this liturgy takes place at another time of year.

The celebrant invites the sponsors to place a hand on the shoulder of the candidate as a sign of their support (454 and 557). This is the same gesture that godparents make at the Rite of Election (133).

Celebration of the Calling to Continuing Conversion: Universal Prayer (Prayer of the Faithful), or Intercessions for the Elect and the Candidates

The universal prayer follows (455), though in the combined rite it carries the title Intercessions for the Elect and the Candidates (558). In the uncombined rite, taking place at a parish Mass, one or more of the suggested petitions may be added to those for the church and the world already prepared for the day. As noted above, the petitions are assigned to a lector, but a non-instituted reader or ordained deacon may read them as usual.

The intentions for the candidates are copied from those composed for the 1988 edition with very few variations. The petitions are given in sense lines for ease of proclamation. The reference to Lent is put in parentheses. The sacrament of "reconciliation" is called the sacrament of "penance," as in the revised title of *The Order of Penance*. The final petition draws its wording from the revised translation of a similar petition in the Rite of Election (134A), as it did in the Rite of Sending (442).

In the combined rite, the rubrics are copied from those pertaining to the unbaptized in the Rite of Election, though they note the inclusion of the baptized candidates among those for whom the community prays. If the combined rite takes place at Mass, and if the universal prayer is to be omitted, then these intercessions include some for the church and the world. In either case, the elect may be dismissed after the intentions (558, see 134).

The celebrant's introduction also comes from the Rite of Election because the Calling to Continuing Conversion has none. It simply adds that candidates are included among those for whom the community prays (558, see 134).

Two alternative sets of petitions are supplied. In the first set (558A), the first petition is the second from 134A, originally composed for the elect, but applied to both groups. The second intention is the first from the same set, and it specifically mentions the elect. The third petition is copied from the 1988 edition and has no equivalent in the uncombined Calling to Continuing Conversion. The petition for the catechists comes from the Rite of Election, as does the petition for godparents, which expands to include the sponsors of the candidates. The final petitions for families, the community, and those held back by doubts come from the Rite of Election.

The entire list of alternative petitions in 558B comes from the Rite of Election, except that the first explicitly adds the candidates for clarity (134B). These seem to have been composed with the upcoming scrutinies in mind, though they are generic enough to apply to anyone observing Lent.

The celebrant concludes the petitions with a prayer copied from the 1988 edition, composed for the church in the United States. That edition carried a heading, "Prayer over the Candidates," which has been removed as there is no similar heading for the prayer that concludes the petitions in the Rite of Election (135).

In the combined rite, this prayer replaces the two options from the 1988 edition, both of which had been taken without significant change from the Rite of Election pertaining to the unbaptized. The new prayer is in two parts (559): The first abbreviates 135B for the elect; and the second, based on the first part, prays for the candidates.

Dismissal of the Elect

If the uncombined rite for candidates takes place outside Mass, all are dismissed (457). If Mass continues, and if catechumens are present, the other usual dismissal options pertain, even though this liturgy does not mention them. If needed, those formulas of dismissal can be found in the combined rite (560), which copies them from the Rite of Election (136).

OCIA 457 does not name the minister who issues the dismissal, but if a deacon has assisted, he would appropriately do it. Otherwise, the dismissal falls to the celebrant.

Celebration of the Eucharist

In the uncombined rite, if Mass continues, and if this is a Sunday or solemnity, the Creed comes next, followed by the preparation of the gifts (458). Normally, the Creed precedes the universal prayer, but on occasions where the petitions form an element of the special liturgy being celebrated, as at a wedding, they remain attached to that ceremony, and the Creed follows.

In the combined rite, the instructions for the Liturgy of the Eucharist are also copied from the Rite of Election (561, see 137). If the universal prayer was not incorporated into the intentions, it concludes the Liturgy of the Word. If Mass continues, and if this is a Sunday or solemnity, the Creed and preparation of the gifts come next. In both the combined and uncombined rites, the Creed may be omitted for "pastoral reasons," which probably means the uncommon length of the Mass.

At cathedrals across the country, the combined rite is commonly celebrated without the Eucharist. However, at its origins, the Rite of Election took place within Mass on the First Sunday of Lent. The Roman Missal therefore includes the presidential prayers for it among the Ritual Masses: a collect, prayer over the offerings, and prayer after Communion. These would replace the usual presidential prayers of the Lent Sunday.

Nonetheless, the rite usually takes place within a service of the Word of God. This happens probably due to the length of the ceremony and the logistical challenges of dismissing a large group of catechumens while the faithful remain for Eucharist with the bishop.

Penitential Rite (Scrutiny)

Candidates in the United States may undergo a penitential rite, which was composed for the 1988 edition. There is no Latin original. It is modeled on the scrutinies for the elect. Faithful to a long tradition, those rites prepare the elect for renouncing sin, accepting Christ, and receiving baptism. Baptized candidates stand outside the circle of those whom tradition has called to the scrutinies. As indicated above, candidates from Eastern Orthodoxy require only a profession of faith and should not be included in this rite (474).

The introductory paragraphs for this penitential rite for the candidates (459–63) are based on those for rites adapted for unbaptized *children* (291–94), which do appear in the Latin original. The title for that section for children is now more accurately translated as "Scrutinies or Penitential Rites" (291). The 1988 edition had translated this into English with the reverse emphasis: "Penitential Rites (Scrutinies)," perhaps diminishing further within the children the fear that the word "scrutiny" could impart. The revisers who created the original typical edition softened the expectations for child catechumens by requiring only one scrutiny and offering "penitential rite" as an alternative title.

The adapted introductory paragraphs for adult candidates borrowed the title "Penitential Rite (Scrutiny)" from the 1988 translation of the rites for children. It remains unchanged. Perhaps this was a felicitous oversight because it places the emphasis on penance rather than on scrutiny. Still, the word "scrutiny" poses problems in ecumenical thought because it could lead some to deduce that the candidates' baptism suffered some serious inadequacies.

During Lent this rite may mark the purification of the baptized but uncatechized adults preparing for sacraments or for reception into the full communion of the church. OCIA 459 called it "a kind of Scrutiny." This explanation is identical to the one in the 1988 edition. However, even calling this "a kind of Scrutiny" is a misnomer because those who are already baptized have passed beyond the stage when scrutinies apply. As a penitential rite, it heals sinners on their way toward the sacraments and the celebration of Easter.

This rite pertains to the final stage of preparation and presumes that the candidates have neared the requirements for fuller life in the community (460). This paragraph also borrows ideas from the scrutiny for unbaptized children of catechetical age, who are entering the final stage of their preparation during Lent (292). However, baptized candidates may be received into the full communion of the church at any time of year. Many of them have already received sufficient catechesis and do not require this penitential rite.

The rite aims to benefit the sponsors and the larger assembly as well, even as it prepares the candidates to celebrate the sacrament of penance before their reception or forthcoming sacraments (461). This idea comes from the scrutiny for children, where the catechetical group of the unbaptized may partake in the formation of baptized Catholic kids preparing for their first confession (293). In the case of adult candidates, they are preparing for their own confession.

The words of the rite have the gospel of the Second Sunday of Lent in mind, largely because that Sunday stands without conflict between the Rite of Election on the First Sunday of Lent and the scrutinies beginning on the Third Sunday. However, this penitential rite may be celebrated on a weekday of Lent or at some other suitable time (462). This paragraph is adapted from OCIA 294 for unbaptized children, which more coherently situates their scrutiny during Lent. Choosing Lent for uncatechized candidates makes some sense if they will be receiving the sacraments of the church at Easter.

The next paragraph, 463, has no parallel in the introductory matter concerning the scrutiny for children because it affirms the difference between the unbaptized and the baptized. Exorcisms in the scrutinies belong to the elect and use images referring to their approaching baptism. Therefore, the celebration of these rites for candidates and for the elect is never combined. Striving as it does to make this distinction in theory, the rite's actions and words nonetheless mimic the structure and content of scrutinies.

Introductory Rites: Greeting and Introduction

The liturgy opens with "Introductory Rites," as in the 1988 edition (464). However, that edition's parallel rite for children used "Liturgy of the Word" for its heading, which now appears in the revised translation as "Introduction of the Rite" (295). That would have made a more coherent heading in the revised edition.

The description of the priest's welcome (464) is adapted from the 1988 edition's rite for unbaptized children (295). The difference in translation is slight, but a more careful preparation of this section of the revised edition would have aligned the presentation of this American rite in OCIA 464 with the revised translation of the Latin original for children in OCIA 295. For example, he could say something like this, depending on who is present:

> Welcome to all who have come for worship today:
> the candidates who are preparing to be received into the
> full communion of the Catholic Church,
> Catholic candidates preparing for the sacraments of confirmation and Communion,
> those who are preparing for the sacrament of penance,
> and those who have come to support them in prayer:
> sponsors, catechists, and concelebrating priests.
> All will hear for themselves the blessed message of the
> forgiveness of sins
> and will praise the mercy of God the Father.

If this rite takes place during Mass, especially a Sunday Mass, one expects this introduction to follow the sign of the cross and greeting, and to precede the penitential act and collect.

However, this rite mysteriously envisions a different sequence. After this greeting, it calls for a song—not the other way around, as usually happens at Mass.

The unusual sequence imitates the start of yet another penitential rite, the non-sacramental celebration found in *The Order of Penance*. There the sample penitential celebrations for children, young people, and the sick (43–73) place the greeting before the song. It appears that the compilers of this rite for the United States borrowed elements not only from the scrutiny for unbaptized children, but also from the penitential celebrations for children—neither of which takes place at Mass, and neither of which directly compares to the formation of adult candidates.

Those same penitential celebrations move from the song to the prayer of the celebrant, which explains why the penitential rite for candidates moves from the song to the collect or other prayer without any mention of the penitential act one usually experiences at Mass (OCIA 465). If the OCIA's penitential celebration for adult uncatechized candidates takes place during Mass, then the structure of the introductory rites from the Order of Mass would govern the sequence of elements: song, greeting, penitential act, collect.

Prayer

For the celebrant's prayer, his first option is the Missal's collect for the Second Sunday of Lent. The second option appears to be freely composed for the 1988 edition and repeated in the revision. It may have been inspired by the prayer in this position from the penitential celebration for young people in *The Order of Penance* (56).

Liturgy of the Word

In the Liturgy of the Word, the readings are those assigned to the Second Sunday of Lent if the celebration takes place on that day. On other days, "appropriate readings from the Lectionary are used" (OCIA 466).

The OCIA does not specify what those other appropriate readings may be. As long as the penitential rite is celebrated on a day that does not exclude the use of a Mass for Various Needs and Occasions, alternate readings may be proclaimed. For example, one could draw from "1. For the Church," "15. For Reconciliation," or "27. For the Remission of Sins." These are permitted on weekdays of Ordinary Time, as well as on optional memorials (GIRM 377). A priest judging some pastoral advantage may select one of these Masses to replace an obligatory memorial, and on certain weekdays of Advent, Christmas, and Easter (GIRM 376).

The homily explains the sacred texts (OCIA 467). The description is adapted from the one for the scrutiny of children (298); however, the words in 467 come completely from the 1988 edition and were not revised in light of the new translation for OCIA 298. The difference is slight: the homily invites all in the assembly—not just the candidates—to repentance and conversion of heart in the light of Lent.

Prayer in Silence

For good or ill, the next part of the penitential rite comes directly from the scrutinies for adults. The only difference is the exchange of the word "candidates" for the word "elect" (468, compared with 152, for example).

The candidates and sponsors come forward to stand before the celebrant. As in the scrutiny, the rite does not indicate how they get there. In practice, the celebrant may feel compelled to invite them forward in his own words. However, in liturgical grammar, such an invitation would come from the deacon, if one is assisting. Nonetheless, the candidates could be instructed beforehand that they come forward on their own after the homily. Or their sponsors may take the lead. If the celebrant has been seated for a period of silent reflection, his change in posture could signal the director of the catechumenate, sponsors, and candidates present to advance into the sanctuary.

The celebrant first asks the faithful to pray in silence for the candidates, and then he follows with a similar request of the candidates themselves. The purpose of the prayer is identical to the purpose of prayer for the unbaptized: that they receive a spirit of repentance, a sense of sin, and the true freedom of the children of God. The last expression draws from Romans 8:21. In the context of a scrutiny, it anticipates baptism, which will admit the elect to the status of the children of God. The baptized candidates have already achieved that status, so the celebrant may wish to make the introduction more precise. For example, he could say something like this:

> My brothers and sisters of this assembly,
> please pray a few moments in silence for these candidates
> that, grateful for their baptism,
> they may obtain a greater sense of sin
> and receive a deeper spirit of repentance
> as they prepare (for their reception into the full communion
> of the church and)
> for their confirmation and Communion.

The celebrant invites the candidates to show their spirit of repentance by bowing or kneeling for a while. In a scrutiny, the elect are asked to do the same.

The American adaptation makes no distinction between the groups in the words and postures of this ceremony. An exorcism inside the scrutiny strengthens the elect through Christ who can set them free from the effects of sin and influence of the devil (144). The elect show their spirit of repentance because they have not yet benefited from the grace of the sacraments, as have the candidates. This penitential rite avoids making this distinction.

Intercessions for the Candidates

Intercessions are made for the candidates (469). If this takes place during Mass, these petitions are combined with those for the church and the world. This differs from the rubric for the intercessions for the elect during a scrutiny (153, for example). There, if this takes place at Mass, all the intentions may be combined, but a distinct set of intentions may instead be offered for the elect. In that case, the elect may be dismissed before the subsequent intercessions of the universal prayer, which more properly engage those who have been baptized in their priestly office of praying for the church and the world.

The celebrant's introduction (469) is based on the one for the penitential rite or scrutiny for children (299). That one prays for the unbaptized children as well as for their baptized friends who will celebrate their first confession at the same service. In both introductions, the celebrant includes in the intentions all present who await the mercy of Christ. The revised English translation takes the introduction from the 1988 edition, without aligning the words to the revised translation of OCIA 299. An introduction such as this would take the revised translation into account:

> My brothers and sisters, let us pray for these candidates (N. and N.),
> whom Christ has already ransomed in baptism
> and who now seek the forgiveness of their sins and the healing of their weakness,
> so that they may be ready
> (to be sealed with the gift of the Father and)
> to be fed at the Lord's table,
> and let us pray for ourselves, who await the mercy of Christ.

The intentions (469) resemble those from the Rite of Sending (442), which in turn are inspired by those in the Rite of Election (134A and B). The first two copy those that open the list in OCIA 469 of the 1988 edition. The next three are taken from the revised translation of the Rite of Election (134B). The following three come again from the 1988 edition, and the final intention for the gathered community comes from the first scrutiny of the unbaptized (153A). The person reading this last intention may omit the reference to the coming of Easter if the rite is celebrated outside Lent.

Concluding Prayer

The celebrant offers a "Concluding Prayer" (470), which the 1988 edition called "Prayer over the Candidates." It replaces the exorcism in the scrutinies (154 and 300, for example). The rubric at 470 still calls it the "Prayer over the Candidates."

The revised English translation introduces the command, "Let us pray" before the prayer, as happens in the scrutinies. Also, as in a scrutiny for the adult elect, the celebrant joins his hands for the prayer to the Father. Then he may impose hands on the candidates before offering a second prayer, this one directed to the Son.

The first option (470A) borrows images from the gospel of the Second Sunday of Lent and is useful on that day. The second option (470B) may be used on other occasions. The revision keeps the words from 1988 edition, making adjustments for capital letters and the concluding formulas of the prayers.

All may sing a suitable song, and the recommended psalms are exactly those from the scrutinies. If the Eucharist is not celebrated, the entire assembly may be dismissed (471).

Dismissal of the Assembly or Celebration of the Eucharist

The 1988 edition assigned the dismissal to the celebrant, in keeping with many examples from the typical edition. The revision does not indicate the speaker of the dismissal, which allows a deacon to say it as he does at the conclusion of Mass.

The 1988 edition permitted the celebration without the Eucharist to conclude with an appropriate song. The 2024 revision oddly permits a suitable chant *before* the dismissal (471)—immediately after the permission for a suitable chant to conclude the previous prayers (470). The permission seems to be copied over from the Rite of Welcoming (432) and the Rite of Sending (444) without noticing the needlessness of another song before the dismissal. This oversight obscures the original intent that a single song precede the dismissal.

If the Eucharist is celebrated, Mass resumes with the Creed when required, or immediately with the preparation of the gifts when it is not (472). As in the Rite of Sending, even when the Creed is required, it may be omitted for pastoral reasons (445). This probably accommodates people feeling inconvenienced by the length of the service, rather than some theological preference for the omission of the Creed.

Confession

The candidate is to celebrate the sacrament of reconciliation before being received into the full communion of the church (482). A priest is authorized to administer this sacrament to a Christian of another denomination under the conditions in DAPNE 130.

Many of those in formation for reception look forward to this opportunity. Whereas some Christians have found confession an obstacle to joining the Catholic Church, others have found the joy of forgiveness one of the most appealing aspects of church life.

The penitent has all of the same options as anyone else: individual confession or a communal service in which participants confess and receive absolution individually, and the choice of confessing anonymously or face-to-face. Usually the most fruitful form is when the candidate makes an appointment with a priest for a confession. This removes the constraints of time that confessors sometimes feel when one penitent requires additional attention while others may be waiting in line. However, candidates may simply join the line of other penitents, await their turn, explain their status as a candidate, and proceed.

Candidates may celebrate this sacrament at any time of their formation—even multiple times. Typically they will want to confess on a day close to that of their reception as part of their immediate preparation.

Conditional Baptism

The church offers caution around the administration of conditional baptisms. In the past, many baptized candidates for reception into the church underwent a conditional baptism. The practice is now discouraged, especially in cases where there is no question about the validity of the baptism already received.

To determine validity, recourse may be made to the diocesan marriage tribunal. If a baptism is deemed valid for the sake of processing an appeal for a decree of nullity, then the same baptism is deemed valid for the sake of reception into the full communion of the Catholic Church. OCIA 480 summarizes the church's thinking:

> The Sacrament of Baptism cannot be repeated, and therefore conditional Baptism is not permitted to be conferred again unless a prudent doubt is present concerning the fact or the validity of the Baptism already conferred. If after a serious investigation has been undertaken concerning the prudent doubt about the fact or validity of the Baptism already conferred, conditional Baptism seems necessary to confer again, the minister should appropriately explain the reasons why Baptism in this case is being conferred conditionally, and he should administer it in a private form.
>
> The local Ordinary should determine in individual cases of conferring conditional Baptism which rites should be kept and which omitted.

The church's reticence is immediately noted. The OCIA does not begin with conditions for administering a conditional baptism, but rather lays out reasons why it may not be permitted.

Conditional baptism requires a "prudent doubt"—not an arbitrary one, or one that has not been adequately researched. The doubt may concern the fact of baptism—whether or not it actually took place. Or it may concern the validity of the baptism—whether the undisputed baptism that happened fulfilled the requirements for validity.

It requires a "serious investigation." Every effort should be made to resolve the doubt so that the person's sacramental status can be established. If a valid baptism took place, then the person may rejoice in it. If it did not, then the person may prepare for absolute baptism, not a conditional one.

OCIA 480 relies on the Ecumenical Directory of 1967 and 1970, which in turn received further clarifications. The 1983 Code of Canon Law restated the same points: the doubt pertains either to the fact or the validity of baptism, and the investigation needs to search out the words and ceremonies of the baptism, as well as the intention of the one baptized and of the minister. The sacrament is administered only after the doctrine of baptism has been explained (c. 869).

The 1993 Ecumenical Directory expresses the same concerns. Conditional baptism is not to be administered "unless, in a particular case, an examination clearly shows that a serious reason exists for having a doubt about one of the following: the matter and form and words used in the conferral of baptism, the intention of an adult baptized or the minister of the baptism" (DAPNE 99c).

If baptism is to be administered conditionally, the local ordinary determines in each case how it is to be done. Certain rites may be included; others not. Before a priest or deacon administers a conditional baptism, he is to consult the ordinary to determine which elements of baptism to include.

Furthermore, the priest or deacon must administer the baptism in private, not in public (OCIA 480). Therefore, it is not to take place at the same time as the baptisms of other adults.

Nor is there a conditional formula to be used, such as, "If you have not been baptized, I baptize you. . . ." Although some priests have been taught to introduce the baptism with these words, they appear nowhere in the OCIA, *The Order of Baptism of Children*, the Code of Canon Law, or the *Catechism of the Catholic Church*. Rather, the minister explains privately to those present why the decision was made for this conditional baptism to take place. That explanation replaces the expression, "If you have not been baptized." The minister baptizes using the traditional formula without adjusting it.

A parallel situation exists in anointing the sick. If the priest doubts whether the person is alive, he anoints the person using the regular formula (135 or 263 in the first English edition)—not, "If you are alive, through this holy anointing. . . ."

In spite of all these restrictions, a survey conducted by the Georgetown's Center for Applied Research in the Apostolate (CARA) showed how widely conditional baptism has been administered. Sixty-one percent of responding parishes practiced at least one conditional baptism in the previous year. Of those, 29 percent performed the ceremony at the Easter Vigil, and another 2 percent at Sunday Mass. The results suggest that parishes practice conditional baptism more broadly than the Vatican's ecumenical offices had hoped, and that priests ignore the preference for using the private form in over 50 percent of the cases.[6] For the sake of the integrity of baptism, these habits should change.

[6] Paul Turner, "The Amen Corner: On Conditional Baptism," *Worship* 91 (January 2017): 4–11.

4

The Order of Reception

Relevant Information

Requirements

The opening paragraph of commentary on the Order of Reception refers to Acts of the Apostles 15:28, a verse from the so-called Council of Jerusalem. The apostles had gathered in Jerusalem to debate the question of baptizing Gentiles without having them first become Jews. For Gentile men, this would have demanded circumcision. St. Paul believed that Gentiles should have direct access to life in Christ, and his view prevailed. The gospel established a new law not requiring a person first to become a Jew in order to follow Christ. The apostles thus created a direct route to baptism. Now the Catholic Church has created a direct route for validly baptized Christians of other denominations to access Christ at the eucharistic table.

Still, some preparation is expected (477). This is to be both doctrinal and spiritual, accommodated to individual cases. Through this preparation the candidates will adhere more lovingly to the church and find in it the fullness of their own baptism.

The formation will also include opportunities for worship as offered by what it calls the Ecumenical Directory (477). As explained above, since the publication of the typical edition in 1972, that directory from 1967 and 1970 has been replaced by the 1993 Directory for the Application of Principles and Norms on Ecumenism. Thus the formation of baptized candidates shares multiple prongs as does that of the unbaptized (75).

Throughout this process, "Equating candidates with catechumens is to be altogether avoided" (477). This ecumenical concern aims to value the baptism of candidates, as well as the mutual sharing of major beliefs among Christians, including the inspiration of the Bible, certain moral imperatives, and aspects of worship. The unbaptized are in a totally different relationship to the church.

Surprisingly, the very next paragraph threatens to mitigate this absolutism by inviting baptized candidates to participate in liturgical rites that parallel those for the unbaptized. This paragraph was added to the 1988 American edition and does not reflect the Latin typical edition's original vision of the reception of Christians. This paragraph allows preliminary rites "for pastoral reasons and in light of the catechesis in the faith" that they previously received (478). Nonetheless, for other pastoral reasons and when previous catechesis has been ample, the original vision of no greater burden than necessary may prevail: candidates may be received without preliminary rites.

Eastern Orthodox Christians

As noted above, for Eastern Orthodox Christians, nothing more is required except a simple profession of the Catholic faith (474). The previous translation declared that "no liturgical rite is required," but the revised translation omits that phrase in keeping with a more accurate translation of the Latin.

Eastern Orthodox baptism generally includes the sacrament of confirmation (chrismation). When a Catholic priest celebrates the Order of Reception for an Eastern Orthodox person, he does not administer confirmation.

The Mass of Reception

Before offering its translation of two observations from the typical edition at OCIA 475, the American edition gives an explanatory introduction that does not appear in Latin: "In regard to the manner of celebrating the Rite of Reception." Copied from the 1988 edition, it mistakenly calls this the "Rite" of Reception, where the title of the ritual has changed to the "Order" of Reception.

The first point stresses the importance of celebrating this step at Mass (475a). In that way the high point of eucharistic Communion is more readily manifest.

The second point stresses the importance of avoiding triumphalism (475b). Consequently, the ceremony may be held in the presence of only a few family and friends.

In practice, many communities celebrate the ritual in the context of Sunday Mass so that members of the parish witness the discernment of the individual and the growth of their numbers. Daily Mass offers another option for those who desire to be received in a small celebration. However, the Order of Reception should normally take place during Mass. Consultation with the one being received is important.

In the event that the reception takes place outside Mass, then the newly received person should take the opportunity to receive the Eucharist at Mass as soon as possible (476). Although it is permissible to receive someone into the full communion of the church without immediate Communion, it incongruously removes the high point of the celebration.

Abjuration of Heresy

In the past, baptized Christians were required to make an abjuration of heresy. This is no longer expected (479). Other Christians are considered brothers and sisters to Catholics. They are not expected to renounce what formed them in Christ. Coming into the full communion of the church happens not through an abjuration of heresy, but through a profession of faith.

Bishop, Priest, Sponsor, Godparent

The bishop is the proper minister for reception. However, a priest entrusted with such duties receives and confirms the candidate—unless the one being received has already been confirmed (481), as is the case in Eastern Orthodoxy.

A sponsor may accompany the one being received. The 1988 translation stated this more strongly: "the candidate should be accompanied by a sponsor." The revised translation faithfully represents the Latin original: "If the situation warrants, a sponsor . . . may accompany the one being admitted in the Reception itself" (483). This optionality is puzzling because the sponsor is mentioned twice in the celebration (490 and 497), and at confirmation a "godparent" must play a role (494).

One possible background for the optionality of a sponsor is a sentence that appeared in *The Order of Confirmation* between the time of its typical edition in 1971 and the publication of the revised English translation in 2016. Number 5 used to tolerate the absence of a sponsor and to have parents present their own children instead. That option has since been removed. A sponsor for confirmation is required. However, the typical edition of the Order of Reception appeared in 1972 when the 1971 confirmation rules were still in force. That may have contributed to a sense that the sponsor was optional.

Another possibility is that OCIA 483 is referring to a sponsor similar to the one in OCIA 10, a person who has known and helped the catechumen, but who may be replaced by a godparent who assists from the Rite of Election forward (11). In the case of the candidate, the sponsor is described as one having "a greater role than others in leading or preparing the candidate" (483). And this sponsor accompanies the candidate "in the Reception itself"—that is, not necessarily in the sacrament of confirmation, when another person could serve.

According to OCIA 494, not the sponsor, but the "godparent" places his or her right hand on the shoulder of the one to be confirmed. The edition in the United States has copied this instruction from the Simpler Order of Adult Initiation, where the person acting as the confirmation sponsor is the godparent who just assisted at baptism (366). In the typical edition, the Order of Reception refers the priest back to the Simpler Order to find the formula for confirmation. The revised translation copies it over here for the ease of the presider. In *The Order of Confirmation* for those baptized Catholic as infants, the person who assists is called a sponsor (OConf 26). OCIA 494 probably should have taken the word "sponsor" from *The Order of Confirmation,* rather than "godparent" from the earlier pages of the OCIA.

If this reading is correct, then more than one sponsor could assist. One may be the person who assisted the long formation of the candidate. Another could be the one who accepts the responsibilities associated with confirmation. Where OCIA 483 permits two sponsors, it probably means two sponsors for the reception, as anyone being baptized may be accompanied by one or two godparents. *The Order of Confirmation* does not explicitly allow a second godparent.

Planning to Receive Holy Communion

During the Mass of reception, communion under both kinds may be administered to the sponsors, parents, spouse, and catechists—indeed to all eligible Catholics present (484). If the Order of Reception takes place outside of Mass, then Communion under both kinds may be administered at the next Mass in which the person participates.

Communion under both kinds is now practiced more widely in the United States than in 1972 when the typical edition was published. This shows a vestige of a previous practice when drinking Communion from the cup was rare. An occasion such as this grew in dignity and celebration when the faithful could drink the Blood of Christ.

Adaptations

The conference of bishops may adapt the rite to various local circumstances (485). Even a local ordinary—without the entire conference—may lengthen or abbreviate the rite if it seems appropriate.

The OCIA gives no examples of this. Abbreviating the rite could assuage the inconvenience of a longer celebration, or it could remove even more of the feared triumphalism in the celebration. Lengthening it could introduce some elements of local interest that would help the new Catholic feel a stronger bond to the diocese.

Records

Following the liturgy, the names of those received are to be recorded in a special book, along with the date and place of their baptism (486). The revised national statutes for initiation call for this in norm 16.

In the United States, these names are to be kept in a parish archive, along with the date and place of birth, the names of the minister, parents, and sponsors, and the date and place of reception into the full communion of the church. The proper execution and care of these records is essential.

In many parishes, the record is kept in the baptismal register because that is the place where most people would go searching for it. Diocesan leadership may determine the appropriate place to keep the record.

Order of Reception into the Full Communion of the Catholic Church of Those Already Validly Baptized

The Choice of the Mass

The reception may be celebrated within or outside Mass. Because the fruit of reception is participation in Holy Communion, the celebration within Mass is preferable.

If the liturgy takes place on a solemnity or a Sunday, the Mass of the day is celebrated. For example, at a parish Mass on a Sunday in Ordinary Time, the priest offers the Missal's prayers of that Mass, and the regular Sunday readings are proclaimed. However, if it takes place on another day, the Mass "For the Unity of Christians" may be used. The priest draws his prayers from the Missal's Masses for Various Needs and Occasions, and the readings come from the same set of Masses in the Lectionary (488).

Although the OCIA permits such a Mass "on other days" (487), those are restricted to days when a Mass for Various Needs and Occasions may be offered: weekdays of Ordinary Time, or, if the need is great, on obligatory memorials, and on other weekdays except those in the weeks preceding and following Christmas and Easter. These rules are explained in the Missal's introduction to its Masses for Various Needs and Occasions.

The Order of Reception may be combined with the initiation of the elect at the Easter Vigil. Although this is commonly practiced, the OCIA first envisions it taking place on a separate occasion. Commentary on the vigil's combined rites is found below.

The Liturgy of the Word

On days when permitted, readings from the Mass "For the Unity of Christians" or the Ritual Mass of Christian Initiation Apart from the Easter Vigil may be proclaimed (OCIA 488). Those for the unity of Christians are found in the fourth volume of the Lectionary among its Masses for Various Needs and Occasions (LM 867–71).

The Old Testament options offer prophecies about the reunification of divided Israel. The New Testament selections treat the theological unity of the church in Christ, set upon the foundation of apostles and prophets; they also address the practicalities of the challenge and beauty of living with other believers in harmony.

The responsorials develop themes of unifying those who are scattered and the joy of a pilgrimage to Jerusalem. Several of the suggested gospel acclamations come from these passages or ones like them, but they include two nonbiblical options. The second of these is inspired by the fifth paragraph of the treatise "On the Unity of the Church" by St. Cyprian (+258). The gospel options reflect Jesus's desire for unity among his followers.

The Mass "For the Unity of Christians" expresses a desire shared by all who follow Christ—that all may be one. However, to insert the reception of Christians at a parish church into the overall intent of this Mass formula looks more unifying to the Catholic side than it may from the perspective of other Christians.

Alternatively, the readings from the Mass for initiation may be used (OCIA 488), but they should not appear to equate this ceremony with the full initiation of the unbaptized. These are also found in the fourth volume of the Lectionary, though among the Ritual Masses (LM 751–54).

The Old Testament options develop the themes of covenant and exodus, or the foreshadowing of the properties of the waters of baptism. The New Testament passages bear testimony to the first baptisms and their meaning. These could be used if they underscore the power of the baptism that the candidate has already received.

The responsorials anticipate the new creation and the impact of the sacraments of initiation on the individual receiving them. The Alleluia verse and verse before the gospel draw from many of the passages in this section. The gospel selections propose discipleship and its expectations, as well as the fruits of baptism.

One should be careful about selecting passages from either of these Masses, so that the nature of the Order of Reception is not misinterpreted. It should not look as though the only way forward to unify those who follow Christ is to have all other Christians become Catholic one by one. The path of ecumenism involves considerable dialogue and mutual understanding.

Oddly, OCIA 488 does not recommend readings from the Lectionary's Ritual Mass for the Reception of Baptized Christians into the Full Communion of the Catholic Church (LM 761–63). Just as strange, these are offered for the Celebration of Reception outside Mass (OCIA 501)—even though the Lectionary is assembled for the purpose of supplying proper readings within Mass.

No Old Testament readings are proposed, and the New Testament options are unique. They propose a variety of themes: predestination as being conformed to the image of God's Son, the love that Christians are to share with one another, God's choice to admit people into union with Christ, the unity of baptism, the call for Christians to meditate on what is pure, and the invitation to rejoice and pray to the God who preserves people for the coming of the Lord Jesus. All of these more directly apply to a Celebration of Reception.

The responsorials summon the themes of light, thirst, refuge, and praise. The gospel choices center on discipleship with its demands and privileges. These selections also more precisely express the nature of the Order of Reception.

The description of the homily provides appropriate direction to the celebrant (489). He is to speak with gratitude about the baptism already received, which is the foundation of the candidate's faith. He also speaks about confirmation, which the candidate has probably not have yet received, and about the upcoming First Communion.

The 1988 translation cast this description in the plural, inviting the homily to consider "those" being received instead of the single candidate indicated in the typical edition. The plural fed the assumption that candidates were to be formed in groups. The typical edition envisioned that they be helped to the table on a more individualized and streamlined process, one by one.

Celebration of Reception: Invitation

The celebrant invites forward both the candidate and the sponsor to profess faith together with the gathered assembly (490). The celebrant may use his own words, but a sample formula is provided. In parishes, the candidate and sponsor are usually seated in the first pew, from which they may more easily approach the sanctuary.

The invitation recalls that the candidate has come freely and after careful discernment. The person has not been forced to profess the Catholic faith. At times in history, people have accused the Catholic Church of compelling unbelievers to be baptized or to switch denominations. The celebrant's declaration distances this ritual from such practices.

The Niceno-Constantinopolitan Creed is always professed at this Mass (491). During Lent and Easter time the Missal now suggests that the Apostles' Creed be proclaimed on Sundays, the church's baptismal Creed (Order of Mass 19). But at this Mass, even during those times of the year, the Nicene Creed, a deeper proclamation that affirms great unity, is required.

The revised American edition has placed the complete text of the Creed here, a feature that the 1988 edition lacked. This keeps the celebrant from switching books if he needs to follow the words. Or, if the priest has the words memorized, a server could turn the ritual book toward the candidate to assist their proclamation of the Creed. This would also put before the eyes of the candidate the words that he or she is to say next: "I believe and profess all that the holy Catholic Church believes, teaches, and proclaims as revealed by God" (491). As noted above in the section on the content of catechesis, that statement has undergone a slight change in the revised translation.

Formula of Reception

If confirmation does not follow because the person received it at their baptism, the celebrant lays hands on the candidate's head. This happens, for example, when receiving a person from an Eastern Orthodox Church. Otherwise the celebrant omits this gesture (492).

The celebrant then announces the formula of reception, formerly called the act of reception (492). The revised translation makes only a few small changes. Instead of saying, "His loving kindness has led you here," the celebrant says of the Lord, "In his mercy he has led you here." It is not knowledge of God's loving kindness alone that has brought the candidate to this day; God himself led the candidate here.

Furthermore, the previous translation had the celebrant say that the candidate may have full communion "in the unity of the Holy Spirit," but the revised, faithful to the Latin, simply says that full communion is "in the Holy Spirit." In the conclusion of the collects at Mass, the phrase "in the unity of the Holy Spirit" refers to the way that the Father and the Son dwell as one with the Holy Spirit. Here, the celebrant's words are declaring that full communion comes in the Holy Spirit—probably a reference to the power of the sacrament of confirmation before the reception of Holy Communion.

Additionally, in place of saying that the candidate professed faith "in the presence of [the Lord's] family," the celebrant says, "before this his family." This surely does not imply that the baptized candidate was not part of the Lord's family before this day, but it rather defines the gathered assembly as the manifestation of the Lord's family into which the candidate is being received. Once the celebrant pronounces all these words of OCIA 492, the candidate has become Catholic.

In the United States, an instruction is inserted here to indicate that the celebrant offers a sign of welcome if the person "is not confirmed" (492). This is very confusing because it means "if the person is not *to be* confirmed," not "if the person has not yet been confirmed." The instruction pertains to one who has been validly confirmed, such as in an Eastern Orthodox Church, and it tells the celebrant to omit conferring the sacrament and bestow the sign of welcome instead. If the candidate has not yet been validly confirmed, as is usually the case, the celebrant administers the sacrament and later gives the sign of welcome.

Celebration of Confirmation: The Laying On of Hands

The priest has the faculty to confirm the candidate whom he receives into the full communion of the church. Not only does he have the faculty, but he must use it (cc. 883 §2 and 885 §2). This is in force no matter the age of the candidate—as young as the age for First Communion and as old as a human can be.

Furthermore, the permission is not restricted to a certain occasion or time of year, such as the Easter Vigil. The faculty pertains to the reception of candidates at every occasion throughout the year. The priest does not require permission from the bishop; he has permission from the law itself, which expects him to exercise it and confirm on any day.

In the United States, the OCIA includes baptized, uncatechized Catholics among those it calls candidates. Such candidates do not undergo the Order of Reception because they are already Catholics. Furthermore, the priest does not have the faculty to confirm them from the law itself. If he receives permission from the bishop to confirm a candidate who had been baptized in the Catholic Church, and if he conducts the ceremony outside the Easter Vigil, he uses *The Order of Confirmation*, not the Order of Reception into the Full Communion of the Catholic Church. Many parishes do not own a copy of *The Order of Confirmation* as it mainly pertains to the office of the bishop. However, there are occasions when a priest needs it.

To administer confirmation in the Order of Reception, the celebrant "lays his hands over the candidate's head" for the prayer (OCIA 493). However, when offering the same prayer for a group of Catholics previously baptized as infants, he "lays hands over all those to be confirmed" (OConf 25). That implies an extension of his hands over the group. In the Order of Reception, though, which imagines a single person being confirmed, the specific mention of the candidate's head implies that the celebrant may lay hands directly on the individual. He makes the same gesture when confirming someone in danger of death (*Pastoral Care of the Sick* 136 and 297).

If the celebrant is confirming a small group of candidates for reception, he could first impose hands individually, and then extend hands over the group for the prayer. However, one should note that the church considers the biblically inspired imposition of hands to be part of the act of *anointing* when the priest is touching the candidate's forehead with his thumb. Pope St. Paul VI made this clear near the end of his apostolic constitution on the sacrament of confirmation.

The words of this prayer have been updated to match those in the 2016 revised English translation of *The Order of Confirmation* (OConf 25). Many celebrants have been using the extra book at this point of the Order of Reception in order to find the appropriate words. For convenience and precision, these are now all in the same book.

The Anointing with Chrism and the Celebrant's Sign of Welcome

For the anointing, the godparent places his or her right hand on the shoulder of the one to be confirmed (494). As noted above, this person is more precisely the "sponsor," but these paragraphs have been copied from the full initiation rites (366), where the baptismal godparent continues as the sponsor for confirmation. In this situation, the newly received person almost certainly did not have a Catholic baptismal godparent. If so and if available, that godparent may serve, but usually this is a different person, the confirmation sponsor.

The celebrant calls the newly received person by name and recites the sacramental formula (494). The instruction implies that he calls the person by their birth or baptismal name. There is no suggestion that a special confirmation name be used at this time. The custom of choosing a confirmation name persists in the United States, but it has no further basis in liturgy or law. The use of the baptismal name more directly links this sacrament to baptism and imitates the formula in other sacraments, such as marriage.

The newly confirmed answers "Amen" to the formula, and the celebrant offers words of peace (494). At Mass, one would expect the celebrant to extend his hands or to shake hands as the faithful frequently do in the pews. However, no gesture is specified to accompany these words. Nonetheless, the very next rubric calls for the celebrant to greet the person, taking their hand in his own in friendship and acceptance (495). In some cultures, another sign of welcome may be more fitting, and the local ordinary may permit it.

Universal Prayer (Prayer of the Faithful)

For the universal prayer, the OCIA provides a sample introduction and intentions (496). As in the 1988 translation, these have been taken from two different places in the typical edition to make them more usable. As with many other parts of the revision, these words now appear in sense lines for ease of proclamation.

Again, the OCIA envisions that a single person has been received at this celebration. The celebrant mentions him or her by name in the introduction. The 1988 edition said that the person had been "united to Christ" through baptism and confirmation; the revision more richly says that the person was "incorporated into Christ" through these sacraments.

The intentions, too, have a more precise revised translation. The first is for the person received, and instead of praying that he or she persevere faithfully in the "choice" that they have made, the intention prays that the new Catholic persevere faithfully in his or her "resolve."

The next two intentions retain their strong ecumenical appeal. They pray for unity among all Christians and for the specific community in which the newly received person has been baptized. The options in this petition are for the "church" or the "community"—indicating either an Eastern Orthodox Church or Western Christian denomination, respectively. Some parishes have warmly and respectfully included the name of the specific congregation that nurtured the Christian faith of the newly received person. For example, the first words of the petition could be crafted, in general or specifically, in imitation of one of these examples:

> For the Evangelical Lutheran Church in America, in which N. was baptized and formed. . . .

> For Hope Lutheran Church, where N. was baptized and formed. . . .

The petitions then pray for nonbelievers who have begun to believe in Christ, and those who do not yet believe. Subsequent petitions pray for world peace and faithfulness among the gathered assembly. All of these intentions are optional, but they show the sweep of values the church embraces at this moment of reception.

Sign of Peace

The sponsor gives a friendly greeting to the newly received person, and others may as well (497). The ritual calls this a sign of peace and permits it to replace the sign of peace before Communion. However, the signs have a different purpose.

This is more specifically noted as a greeting, a welcome that the members of the local church may share with the new member. The sign of peace before Communion expresses the peace and unity that exists among all the same members as they prepare for their sacramental Communion. Both may fittingly be retained.

The order of service does not explain how the community is invited to greet the newly received. In practice, a deacon or the priest would appropriately walk the person to an accessible space, such as the central Communion station, and then invite forward any members of the assembly who wish to join this act. In practice, a procession similar to the Communion procession may take shape: The newly received person may stand in the nave at the center of the main aisle near the sanctuary, and members of the congregation may approach to offer their own spontaneous words of welcome and peace. The priest or a deacon may introduce this action with words such as these:

> Many of you probably wish to share your joy with N. I invite you forward now to offer (him/her) a sign of peace and welcome.

After the last person has offered a sign of welcome, the new Catholic returns to the pews for the remainder of the Mass. However, it would be appropriate for the newly received to assist in the procession of the gifts. That bread and wine will be prepared, consecrated, offered, and returned to the faithful—including the newly received—as the Body and Blood of Christ.

Celebration of the Eucharist

As Mass continues, the newly received person receives Holy Communion for the first time as a Catholic. As indicated above, Communion under both kinds is especially appropriate (498), as would be receiving the Body of Christ from the bread consecrated at this Mass (GIRM 85).

The order of service does not include a special invitation to Communion, as takes place in the combined rite (OCIA 594). The OCIA and the missal expect the celebrant to offer final catechesis to the newly baptized before receiving their First Communion, and the edition in the United States scripts a suggested formula (243).

The combined rite for the Easter Vigil expands that formula to include the newly received. It could be argued that this is an overreach; after all, the newly baptized are the ones completing their initiation that night, and their period of catechesis comes to fruition as the celebrant offers these words in the moments before their First Communion. The order of service for baptized Christians has always taken a more subdued approach to this moment, keeping its ritual focus on the elements pertaining directly to the reception and confirmation of candidates.

However, the sample formula at OCIA 594 will probably appeal to some priests wanting to call attention to this moment, in imitation of the Communion of the newly baptized. For example, the celebrant could say something like these words:

> N., you are now completing your Christian initiation
> and will partake in this most Blessed Sacrament.
> May the Body and Blood of Christ the Lord
> help you grow deeper in his friendship
> and in communion with the entire church;
> may it be your constant food for the journey of life
> and a foretaste of the eternal banquet of heaven.
> Behold the Lamb of God. . . .

One should nevertheless exercise caution. Such an innovation should not lead others to interpret a certain equivalence between catechumens and candidates.

Order of Reception outside Mass

Reception may take place outside Mass (499–504). This should only happen for an unspecified "serious reason." In even more "extraordinary circumstances" the celebration may omit the entire Liturgy of the Word. In that case a simple quotation from the Bible is used to praise the mercy of God and to anticipate eucharistic Communion at a later date. The reasons could include a serious illness or the inaccessibility of the requisites for Mass.

The celebrant does not wear the usual vestments for Mass. He wears an alb or cassock and surplice, as well as a stole of festive color (500). The rubric does not mention that the priest may wear a cope; this omission could be an oversight, or it could indicate the urgent circumstances surrounding this ceremony.

The celebrant's greeting is mentioned before the singing of a suitable song (500–501). Perhaps he is to begin informally without a procession of ministers—in a hospital room, for example.

A suggested selection of readings comes from the New Testament, psalms, and gospels (501). As noted above, the fourth volume of the Lectionary devotes a special section to these, which focus on themes of baptism, discipleship, and unity. OCIA 501 allows for the reading of a single biblical passage, but more may be used. These are explained in the homily, presumably given by the celebrant.

The Order of Reception takes place as described in 489–95. No further guidelines appear in this version of the ritual without Mass (502).

To introduce the universal prayer, the celebrant mentions the sacraments of initiation and the community's gratitude to God. He may use the introduction from the order of service within Mass (503, citing 496).

The first suggested petition mentions the person who has been received (503). The others may come from those proposed for the order of service that includes the celebration at Mass (496). Or someone may compose a set of intentions unique to this celebration.

At any Mass, the celebrant alone concludes the universal prayer with words addressed to God. In this case, because the Liturgy of the Eucharist does not follow, the recitation of the Lord's Prayer in common replaces the celebrant's concluding prayer (504). He concludes the petitions at a wedding without Mass in the same way (*The Order of Celebrating Matrimony* 103A).

If the newly received has been accustomed to concluding the Lord's Prayer with the doxology that begins, "For the kingdom," it may be added here (504). If the reception had taken place at Mass, these words would have been proclaimed in the usual place.

The celebrant gives a blessing, probably one inspired by those from the Missal. This could be a simple blessing, a prayer over the people, or a solemn blessing. OCIA 504 offers no preference.

The sponsor and others may give a friendly greeting to the newly received. All then depart in peace (504), apparently without a formula of dismissal. This again suggests the informal and urgent nature of this particular celebration outside Mass.

One could envision a situation when the celebration within Mass on a particular day may be difficult—as on Ash Wednesday or Christmas, or because the person to be received requested a more private ceremony. In that case, the Order of Reception outside Mass could be celebrated on the same day that the newly received Catholic will also participate at Mass. Then, without special attention, he or she could receive First Communion.

5

The Combined Rites at the Easter Vigil

Preliminaries

This section of the revised English edition for the United States copies much of the material from the previous one. Greater attention can be given to the individual candidates if they are received into the full communion of the church apart from the Easter Vigil, but this version of the celebration is much practiced throughout the country.

Just above OCIA 562, the very title of this section copies the one from the 1988 edition. The ceremony for candidates is mistakenly called the "Rite" of Reception, not the revised translation's "Order" of Reception.

The introductory paragraph declares that unspecified "pastoral considerations" may lead to including the reception of candidates into the Easter Vigil (562). This probably alludes to the common formation they undertook with the unbaptized, or the occasional situation when unbaptized and previously baptized members of the same family are joining the church.

The only change to this paragraph from the previous edition is the inclusion of unbaptized infants among those who may be present for the Easter Vigil. OCIA 562 refers the reader to *The Order of Baptism of Children* (OBC 28.1), but the third edition of the Roman Missal itself now provides direction for this possibility in its presentation of the Easter Vigil.

The subsequent paragraph leaves unchanged the previous edition's rationale for creating this order of service (OCIA 563), which does not exist in the Latin typical edition. While acknowledging that "the elect will enter the Paschal Mystery through Baptism, Confirmation, and the Eucharist," this paragraph declares that the reception of candidates at the Easter Vigil provides them "a privileged opportunity to recall and reaffirm their own Baptism." However, the recollection and reaffirmation of baptism is something that faithful Catholics do at every Easter Vigil. After concluding the penances of Lent, they renew their baptismal promises at Easter.

The same paragraph argues that receiving the sacrament of confirmation at the vigil shows its connection to baptism. However, that connection has been strengthened in the very administration of confirmation, no matter when it is celebrated. For example, the baptismal godparent may return as the confirmation sponsor, and the candidates renew their baptismal promises.

OCIA 563 further states that baptism points to eucharistic Communion, but this can be affirmed at a reception taking place at any Mass. Previously baptized persons may approach the Communion table when they're ready.

Reception is supposed to avoid "an air of triumphalism" (475b), yet the Easter Vigil is one of the most triumphalist liturgies of the year. Even so, the OCIA permits reception at the vigil for pastoral considerations and refers the reader to its section on the Easter Vigil for theological and liturgical information (564, citing 206–17).

As when reception is celebrated apart from the vigil, the determination of the appropriate occasion is to be made with the candidates (564, citing 475.2). Ecumenical values, local conditions, and personal and family preferences are all cited as criteria. If the combined rite is chosen, the distinction between the unbaptized and the baptized is to be made very clear (565, citing 477).

Celebration at the Easter Vigil of the Sacraments of Initiation and the Order of Reception

Introductory Rites and Liturgy of the Word

The distinction of baptismal status should be manifest by the very seats that the two groups occupy (566). The candidates are to sit apart from the elect, who are called forward for baptism.

In some parishes, the distinction is mistakenly made even earlier. As the celebrant blesses the fire for the paschal candle at the start of the vigil, all are to hold individual candles. Yet ministers in some parishes do not distribute candles to the unbaptized, reasoning that they will receive candles after their baptism. However, there is no rubric calling for such a distinction at the blessing of the fire. Instead, the Missal calls for candles to be prepared for all who participate (RM, the Easter Vigil in the Holy Night, 7). Indeed, the candles held by the faithful are more a sign of the resurrection of Christ the light than of their own personal baptism. Arguably, the meaning of the candles held by the faithful changes later in the vigil when the faithful renew their baptismal promises (OCIA 237, 580).

The homily is to include references to the initiation sacraments and to the Order of Reception (566). When the elect alone are receiving sacraments at the Easter Vigil, no such direction is given to the homilist (218). He is free to preach about Easter. However, the combined rite draws a recommendation pertaining to the homily in the Order of Reception at some other Mass. It proposes various themes, including gratitude to God, the baptism that the candidate has already received, confirmation, and the Eucharist (489). Those homily guidelines have been expanded and carried into the rubrics for the combined rites at the Easter Vigil in the United States.

Celebration of Baptism

The vigil continues with the celebration of baptism (567, see 218). The 2024 English edition offers a new introduction to help the congregation thread its way through the upcoming rituals. Addressing the assembly as "dear friends," the celebrant welcomes the diverse groups to the sacraments and thanks God for them. These categories begin with the elect and infants to be baptized.

Presentation of Those to Be Baptized

The procedures that follow depend on the location of the font—whether it is nearby, a procession away, or in the sanctuary. The 1988 edition referred to the first group as "candidates for baptism," but the revision calls them "those to be baptized" (568, see 219). The change in expression demonstrates a preference that the word "candidates" in this ritual book consistently refer to adults with a valid baptism in another Christian denomination, or uncatechized, adult Catholics. As indicated above, it no longer is used for those who are not yet catechumens or for the elect approaching baptism.

The first option for the Presentation of Those to Be Baptized (568A) considers a situation where the font is close at hand. It removes the instruction for the priest to go there (219A), presumably because he is already there or a few steps away. The combined rite adds information about small children, carried by parents and godparents, as indicated in the Roman Missal's treatment of the Easter Vigil (RM 38). The litany may be introduced and sung once these individuals gather, or while they gather, depending on the size of the group (OCIA 568A).

The second option (568B, see 219B) involves a procession to a font, during which the litany is sung. The combined rite adds the same information from the Roman Missal's Easter Vigil about the placement of any infants to be baptized along with their parents and godparents (RM 38).

The third option (568C, see 219C) covers the circumstance when the font is in the sanctuary. A temporary vessel with water may be prepared beforehand (567, see 218), especially appropriate for those places where the permanent font is in a more secluded area of the church, not visible to a full congregation. The OCIA in the United States draws its description from the Roman Missal's treatment of the Easter Vigil (RM 37). As with the other options, it adds the Missal's information about infants to be baptized.

Celebrant's Instruction

The celebrant invites the faithful to pray for those seeking baptism, that they hold fast to the faith they profess, renewed by the Holy Spirit. He also prays for any infants about to be baptized (569).

The part concerning adults comes from the initiation rites when no candidates are being received (220), which offers an alternative formula not copied into the combined rite. However, the celebrant uses these or similar words, so he is free to use or adapt either instruction.

Litany

The 1988 translation more expansively and colloquially called the next event the "Litany of the Saints," but the revision simply calls it the "Litany" (570). In general, the official ritual books of the Roman Rite avoid the better-known title, "Litany of the Saints." In the rites of ordination, for example, this composition is called a litany of supplication. Although the saints will be invoked, the full litany also includes petitions made to Christ.

All stand for the litany during Easter time. The list of names may expand to include the patron saint of the parish church, of the place (such as the city where the church sits if it was named for a saint), and of those to be baptized (570, see 221). Ideally, these additional saints are inserted in their proper place: biblical figures, early martyrs, Doctors of the Church, founders of religious orders, and more recent saints of inspiration—all arranged in chronological order, and all groups first listing men and then women. The research takes a little time, but putting the saints in proper order shows respect for their lives and for the liturgical tradition.

The patron saints of the candidates are not included in this list of options. The litany is preparing for the baptism of the elect, as the closing petition makes clear, asking God to bring them to new birth through their baptism. The candidates sing the litany in concert with the baptized Catholics present, all praying for those to be baptized.

The priest concludes the litany with a prayer. This prayer, found in the Roman Missal, was missing from the Latin typical edition of the OCIA and therefore from the 1988 English translation. Since then, the celebrant following the baptismal liturgy in his 1988 RCIA maddeningly had to refer back to the Missal to locate this single prayer, or put a copy of it inside the book he used for baptism. Now the revised English translation helpfully copies the prayer from the Missal directly into the OCIA, in both the combined and uncombined rites (570, see 221).

Blessing of Water

The celebrant turns toward the font and extends his hands (571, see 222). The Roman Missal's treatment of the Easter Vigil notes the extension of the priest's hands (RM 44, 46); that gesture is now helpfully brought into the revised English translation. This lengthy prayer, rich in elegance and antiquity, may be replaced by another formula that elicits more of the people's active participation with acclamations (OCIA 222B and C).

At its conclusion the people sing an acclamation taken from the book of Daniel, inviting the springs of water to bless the

Lord (571). This acclamation comes from the Missal and has not previously been found in the English translation of the OCIA; the revised edition helpfully includes it.

Profession of Faith: Renunciation of Sin, Profession of Faith

The elect renounce sin and profess their faith in the Trinity (572–74, see 223–25). Although the Roman Missal indicates that they are anointed with the oil of catechumens, that anointing is omitted on this occasion in the United States, according to particular law (33.7). Catechumens are best anointed during the period of the catechumenate, or even during the period of purification and enlightenment, and they may be anointed more than once (89, 98, and 100). However, they are not to be anointed during the day on Holy Saturday or at the Easter Vigil in the United States.

Rite of Baptism

In the baptism of children, the baptismal promises conclude with the celebrant's declaration they represent the faith of the church, which all are proud to profess in Christ Jesus (OBC 59). That affirmation and the community's "Amen" are omitted at the Easter Vigil (OBC 28 §2).

The elect are baptized by either immersion or pouring (OCIA 575, see 226). The same is true of any infants to be baptized at the vigil, and the Missal now accounts for their presence (RM 50).

The revised edition of the OCIA's combined rite adds the question requesting the parents to declare that the baptism of their child is their will. The same paragraph offers baptismal instructions for infants (575). These paragraphs save providing the priest a copy of *The Order of Baptism of Children* while using the OCIA at this point of the vigil.

Explanatory Rites: Anointing after Baptism

Newly baptized infants are to be anointed on the crown of the head with chrism (577). The same would apply to the highly unusual circumstance when a newly baptized adult or child of catechetical age is not confirmed (577, see 228, both citing 215).

This anointing differs from confirmation. It unites one to the priesthood of Christ, whereas confirmation fills one with the gifts of the Spirit. Still, because the two anointings use the same oil, chrism, the one of lesser importance is omitted for those adults about to be confirmed.

Clothing with a White Garment

The newly baptized are clothed with a white garment, unless this is omitted (578, see 229). The rubrics do not explain what circumstances may cause the omission of handing on this garment. It may allow for variations in local cultures around the world where a white garment bears little significance. That explanation is more plausible than creating an opportunity for omitting one baptismal symbol in order to save time.

Many infants come to their baptism already dressed in white. There are several ways to handle the circumstance. Parents may dress their children in something else, so that they may clothe the children with the white baptismal garment at this time. Or the children may be given a symbolic white garment in addition to what they are wearing. Or the priest may simply indicate the white garments that the children already have on.

Handing On of a Lighted Candle

The newly baptized receive a lighted candle, presented by the godparent (579). The OCIA, which primarily concerns adults, does not acknowledge the special situation of infants (230, 579). Obviously, the godparent cannot place a candle into the hands of a newly baptized infant. One may think that the godparent would keep holding the infant's candle as commonly is done outside the vigil. However, *The Order of Baptism of Children* states without explanation that the handing on of the lighted candle to newly baptized children is omitted at the vigil (OBC 28 §3).

The Missal's treatment of the Easter Vigil says that the candles of the newly baptized are lighted (RM 51), making no distinction between adults and children, which may override the OBC. Indeed, the Missal then explains that the Ephphatha Rite for children, which normally follows their baptism (OBC 65), is omitted at the vigil (RM 51, see OBC 28 §3). The Missal could therefore have noted the omission of lighting candles for children, but it does not.

Perhaps the Missal means to distinguish the lighting of the candle from the handing on of the candle. However, in the case of infants, this ritual is called "Handing On of a Lighted Candle" (OBC 64) even when, outside the vigil, the godparent does not actually present the candle to the infant. In practice, the celebrant will probably oversee the lighting of candles for infants as the Missal seems to presume.

Renewal of Baptismal Promises: Invitation, Renunciation of Sin, Profession of Faith, and Sprinkling of Baptismal Water

All renew their baptismal promises unless they have done so when those to be baptized made theirs (580). These instructions are copied from the Missal (RM 49). A further note unique to OCIA 580 states that the baptized candidates for reception renew their baptismal promises together with the rest of the faithful.

Separating the profession of faith of the elect from the renewal of baptismal promises by the faithful has some advantages. Several of the rites throughout Lent have been leading to this moment: the handing on of the Creed, the scrutinies with their exorcisms, and the recitation of the Creed among the Rites of Immediate Preparation. When the elect respond individually to the questions of renunciation and profession, they bring their newfound faith to its personal and most dramatic expression. This is obscured when all the faithful renew their promises at the same time, though it is permitted.

On the other hand, combining the profession of faith with the renewal of promises avoids the incongruous situation in which the newly baptized, now among the faithful, are immediately invited to *renew* their baptismal promises together with the candidates and the rest of the assembly.

The sprinkling with baptismal water follows the renewal of promises. However, it may follow the explanatory rites, depending on when the faithful renew their promises (583).

Celebration of Reception: Invitation

The reception of the candidates takes place before the newly baptized are confirmed so that both groups can be confirmed at once. Deferring confirmation for the newly baptized has the unfortunate consequence of creating some ritual distance between baptism and confirmation, something that OCIA 215 intended to strengthen. Instead of letting the newly baptized experience their confirmation immediately, they must await the reception of the candidates.

Reception is to take place in the sanctuary. If necessary, the newly baptized, godparents, and parents move to appropriate places—back to the sanctuary for those awaiting confirmation, or back to the pews for infants with their parents and godparents (584, see 231). If a procession from the font to the sanctuary is required, all may sing something appropriate, as the Missal suggests during the sprinkling (RM 56).

A new invitation appears in OCIA 584, in which the celebrant helps the congregation understand the purpose of the upcoming ceremonies. He introduces the Order of Reception of validly baptized Christians wishing to profess the Catholic faith.

Profession by the Candidates and Formula of Reception

The ceremony that follows (584–86) is the reception of several candidates. It is based on the reception of an individual candidate that may take place at other times of year (490–92). The above commentary on these rites also applies here.

However, the communal profession of the Nicene Creed, "which is always said at this Mass" (491), is omitted because of the renewal of baptismal promises that took place before the sprinkling—and perhaps even before the baptism of the elect. The close proximity between the Nicene Creed and the profession of the candidates' faith in what the Catholic Church holds is broken when the combined rites are celebrated at the Easter Vigil.

Celebration of Confirmation

Before confirmation, the congregation may sing a suitable chant (587). This instruction also appeared in the 1988 edition at 231, where it introduced confirmation at the Easter Vigil when no candidates were being received. In the revised translation, 231 has been rewritten to remove the option of celebrating confirmation at the font. The Missal required this change (RM 53). The option for singing a song probably should have remained in 231, as it does in 587.

If the bishop was present to baptize, he administers confirmation. In his absence, the priest who conferred baptism confirms (588, see 232). This strengthens the previous translation, which noted that the priest is authorized to confirm. That comes from canon 866, but canons 883 §2 and 885 §2 oblige the priest to confirm in this instance. If a great many are to be confirmed, a bishop may grant permission for other priests to assist (588, see 232).

If the group of candidates includes some baptized as Catholic who were uncatechized and never received confirmation nor Communion, they join the group to be confirmed (588). Another introduction, new to the revised translation, appears to help the people understand what will transpire.

The celebrant gives the information, which includes the name of the bishop who has given him permission to confirm the Catholics. This reminds the priest that he needs to secure that permission, and it assures the people that he has it. This introduction appears only in this combined rite because of the many categories of people about to be confirmed: the newly baptized, those previously baptized in other denominations, and those baptized Catholic.

The celebrant or some other minister invites those Catholics by name to come forward with their sponsors (588). This invitation is new to this combined rite. Before their baptism, the elect were called forward (568, see 219); that rubric does not specify that the elect be called by name, but in practice they often are. Of course, they are named one by one in the formula of baptism. Those to be received are called by name when the celebrant invites them and their sponsors into the sanctuary (584, see 490). Calling the names of the third group offers them similar dignity.

The invitation to step forward can be made very simply because the celebrant has just explained who the group is. For example, a deacon may say words such as these:

> Would the following Catholic candidates for confirmation please step forward together with your sponsors: N. and N.?

Invitation, the Laying On of Hands, the Anointing with Chrism

All those to be confirmed stand before the celebrant: the newly baptized, the newly received, and the recently catechized Catholics (589). The celebrant addresses them as "candidates for Confirmation." Here alone, the word "candidate" does not refer to those aspiring to be received into the church, but to those who have prepared for confirmation. The term comes from *The Order of Confirmation* and is appropriately put in place here.

The celebrant's address copies the one he would give the newly baptized at the vigil (233), except for the way he addresses the group. The address is inspired by some of the themes suggested for the homily at a confirmation (OConf 22). His words inviting the prayer of the people are slightly adapted from *The Order of Confirmation* (OConf 24). The laying on of hands and anointing with chrism take place as usual (OCIA 590–91, see 234–35 and 493–94).

The newly confirmed are led to their place among the faithful, accompanied by their godparents and sponsors (591). When there are no candidates at the Easter Vigil, the newly baptized remain in the sanctuary for the renewal of baptismal promises by the congregation and then take their places among the faithful (236).

When the reception takes place apart from the vigil, the newly confirmed receive a sign of welcome from the celebrant (495) and remain in place through the universal prayer. Those present may greet the newly received person in a friendly manner before he or she returns to a place among the faithful (497). That greeting by members of the assembly is omitted from the rubrics at the Easter Vigil.

Celebration of the Eucharist

The Creed is omitted due to the making and renewing of baptismal promises. All the newly confirmed take part in the universal prayer from their places in the assembly (592).

For the procession of the gifts, the newly baptized adults or the parents of newly baptized children appropriately carry the gifts to the altar. Full participation in the prayer of the faithful and in the procession of the gifts is new for the newly baptized. The candidates have long shared these privileges.

During the eucharistic prayer, the newly baptized are mentioned collectively, but the newly received and confirmed are not (593). The Missal offers special inserts in the four main eucharistic prayers in its Ritual Masses for Baptism and for Confirmation. In this case, given the link between baptism and resurrection, the intentions pertaining to baptism are used. The eucharistic prayer therefore does not include a special petition for candidates, as it does not in the uncombined Order of Reception. Although some may discern this as a slight, it actually affirms their previous rightful place among those offering this prayer together with the priest.

At Communion, all those celebrating sacraments may receive under both kinds (594). The initiation rites have long asked the celebrant to give a final instruction on the Eucharist before the newly baptized receive for the first time. The revised edition now includes a recommended formula (594, see 243). It is based on the one that recent popes have been saying in Italian at the Vatican's Easter Vigil. It appears in print in English for the first time.

Even more, the edition in the United States has expanded the introduction within the combined rite to include a reference to those previously baptized who are completing their initiation sacraments in Holy Communion. When standing at the altar before Communion, the priest will need not only the missal, but also the OCIA.

6

Concluding Thoughts

The Confirmation of Baptized, Uncatechized Catholics

If baptized Catholics had received either confirmation or First Communion, though not both, the church presumes that they had some formation. To receive the other sacrament, all they need is appropriate formation for it.

Consequently, baptized Catholics who lack only confirmation or First Communion are not included among those whom the American edition of the OCIA calls the candidates. They do not participate in the Rite of Welcoming, the Rites of Handing On, nor the Sending and Calling to Continuing Conversion often held in conjunction with the Rite of Election. Nor do they participate in the optional Penitential Rite (Scrutiny) offered other baptized candidates. However, in 1973 the Congregation for Divine Worship included in the group of uncatechized Catholics some who lacked only confirmation, as can be seen from the material in the appendix of this book.

The bishop is the ordinary minister of the confirmation of those baptized Catholic. Each bishop may determine how he wishes to offer the sacrament. Some bishops include adults in confirmation ceremonies for younger candidates; others gather adults for a special celebration of the sacrament. If Catholic adults lack only First Communion, they may receive it at any Mass after appropriate formation, usually at the parish.

As noted above, to confirm a baptized, uncatechized adult Catholic, a priest requires permission from the bishop. Some bishops have particular law that pre-authorizes priests to confirm such Catholics, but ordinarily the priest requires special permission because he does not have the faculty from universal law for this situation (409). Without it, he has no authority to confirm. In such a case, the OCIA urges the conferral of confirmation "as soon as possible, and indeed, insofar as it is possible, during Easter time" (409).

The priest is also cautioned not to include the Celebration of Reception in the liturgical rites for these Catholics (490–92). He does not invite the Catholic candidates to "profess the Catholic faith" (490). They do not conclude the Nicene Creed with a statement that they "believe and profess all that the holy Catholic Church believes" (491). The priest does not declare that "the Lord receives you into the Catholic Church" (492). They do not receive a sign of welcome from the celebrant or from the community (492, 497). They are already Catholic. None of these statements and actions applies to them.

If the baptized Catholic is to receive sacraments outside the Easter Vigil, and if there are no candidates from other denominations involved, the ceremony to follow is *The Order of Confirmation*. The priest, having obtained permission from the bishop to confirm, conducts that liturgy. Assuming that this takes place during Mass, the newly confirmed Catholic also receives First Communion.

The liturgy could take place outside Mass, again using the pertinent section of *The Order of Confirmation*. However, as confirmation and First Communion are considered sacraments of initiation, their conferral during the celebration of Mass provides their most authentic expression.

After the liturgy, the confirmation of the Catholic is to be recorded in the parish register. It is essential to maintain the accuracy of these records for the sake of the individuals involved.

Evaluating the Combined Rites at the Easter Vigil

Although the revised translation for the United States still permits a combined rite, there are reasons to celebrate the reception of previously baptized Christians apart from the Easter Vigil. These include the meaning of the vigil, the purpose of reception, and the pastoral needs of the parish.

The Easter Vigil

The purpose of the Easter Vigil is to celebrate the resurrection of Christ. Yet in many parishes it has become a kind of "new members night."

The number of those wishing to join the Catholic Church provides joy to the community, but it has borne some consequences. The length of the rites of baptism, reception, and confirmation has discouraged some Catholics from participating in the vigil, especially if they perceive it as a night that pertains more to the private celebrations of families celebrating sacraments.

The vigil, however, is the first celebration of the resurrection. The lighting of the fire, the proclamation of the *Exsultet*, the singing of the Gloria, the return of the Alleluia, the first proclamation of the gospel of the resurrection, and the first reception of the Real Presence of the risen Christ in the sacrament of Holy Communion are all elements that should draw faithful Catholics eagerly to the vigil every year.

Into this tapestry neatly fits the sacrament of baptism, through which the fruits of the resurrection of Christ become manifest in individuals and in the church. The same Catholics who prefer to celebrate Christmas on the eve of the birth of Christ tend to avoid celebrating Easter on the eve of the resurrection of Christ. There's nothing wrong with celebrating Easter on the day of the resurrection, but the Easter Vigil inaugurates Easter far more powerfully than the Christmas Vigil inaugurates Christmas.

Celebrating the Order of Reception apart from the Easter Vigil reduces the number of those celebrating sacraments during that special Mass. This practical consideration could bear fruit in a couple of different ways, especially in the American culture, where a lengthy service may cause tedium.

When the number of initiates is large, those planning the celebration tend to exercise certain options that abbreviate the rest of the service, notably the number of readings. The Missal encourages the proclamation of all nine readings for the sake of the vigil, but more widespread is the practice of reducing the number to the minimum that the vigil permits—such as choosing the shorter form of the first reading from Genesis about the creation of the world, which sets the stage for the new creation coming about through the resurrection of Christ and the sacrament of baptism. By celebrating reception on other days, the entire liturgy of the vigil is held in better balance.

The Purpose of Reception

That balance links more naturally the images of resurrection, baptism, and spring—in the Northern Hemisphere. There the symbols of new life cohere without introducing ceremonies for those already baptized. The OCIA in the United States holds that reception at the vigil "provides the candidates with a privileged opportunity to recall and affirm their own Baptism" (563), but the Catholic faithful are all doing the same.

The combined rites at the vigil introduce infelicities for both the unbaptized and the baptized. For the baptized, the intimate link between their baptism and confirmation is interrupted by the renewal of promises, the sprinkling of the faithful, the reception of those previously baptized, and the introduction of baptized, previously uncatechized Catholics. Those being received do not recite the Nicene Creed in union with the community, and their words of professing what the Catholic Church believes is separated from the renewal of their baptismal promises by the sprinkling rite. The sign of welcome by the faithful is omitted. These accommodations are necessary to fit the rituals into the same ceremony, but the separation of certain elements diminishes some of the impact of the rites.

Pastoral Advantages

Furthermore, when the reception of baptized Christians takes place at other occasions throughout the year, such as a typical Sunday Mass when the faithful have gathered, more members of the community are likely to experience the growth of the church.

Few Catholics are participating in the Easter Vigil, which is a problem that begs for remedy. Greater numbers participate at Sunday Mass. They can share in the joy of new members of the church when the Order of Reception takes place on various occasions throughout the year.

The faithful who witness this liturgy will have a personal experience of the reception of baptized Christians. When they discuss their beliefs with their friends, they become able to give testimony about the ritual through which a Christian of another denomination is received into the Catholic Church at a Mass that includes their confirmation and First Communion. Celebrating reception apart from the vigil is therefore an evangelical tool placed in the hands of ordinary Catholics.

As more Catholics witness the Order of Reception, they become better equipped to engage in conversation with others. When they ask, "Do you have a church?" they know one way to steer the conversation. They can better explain to their neighbors what the Catholic Church offers and what it means when the priest declares that another Christian may now have "full communion with us."

Appendix

In 1973, just one year after the Holy See published the revised rites of adult initiation, *Notitiae,* the journal of the Congregation for Divine Worship, presented some material on applying the initiation rites to uncatechized, baptized adult Catholics. At the time, the congregation was more aware of the need to provide pastoral care by means of ritual adaptations for this group, rather than for Christians validly baptized in other denominations. The articles are noteworthy for the spirit of adaptation that they fostered among local communities. They may well have influenced the development of the adapted rites for baptized candidates in the United States.

Below is copied *Notitiae*'s own summary in English, as it appeared in the early pages of volume 9, numbers 7–8. Summaries also were given in French, Spanish, and German.

Beneath that is an English translation of the reflections, published in Italian, which opened with an explanatory paragraph in Latin. These make available a response that the congregation had given to a question from Cardinal Ugo Poletti, the new Vicar of Rome.

A commentary on these reflections follows, also originally in Italian, and published in the same volume of *Notitiae.* These are signed only with the initials "G. P."

All of this material refers to chapter IV of the typical edition. Much of that material is now in chapter V in the United States. For a proper understanding, it is important to recall that chapter IV of the typical edition dealt only with baptized, uncatechized Catholics. Baptized Christians of other denominations were received directly into the full communion of the church when they completed their formation; there were no parallel paragraphs pertaining to their formation in the typical edition. Nor did this early material offer advice on adapting rites for them.

Summary: Activity of the Congregation of Worship

Reflection on chapter IV of the "Ordo initiationis christianae adultorum." This chapter presents pastoral suggestions for the preparation of Confirmation and Eucharist of the person already baptized and instructed in the faith. To this situation is paralleled that of the person who wishes to deepen his faith and his links with the Christian community and also of the person who lapsed and wishes to take up the practice of his faith again. To give a more concrete and incisive quality to this catechesis, people often want to use the catechumenate method. It has been asked however, which rites of the catechumenate can be used for those already baptized. The catechesis should be based above all on the method of the progressive catechumenate, adapted to the spiritual state of the candidate, using the biblical catechesis offered, and characterized by certain rites. But one can never put the baptized on the same level as the non-baptized. Baptism can never be repeated. Therefore something similar to the catechumenate can be adopted for the baptized, but the catechumenate itself may not be used. Some elements may be used: liturgy of the word, blesings [*sic*], rites of passage, while others, those received in baptism cannot be repeated but could be "recalled."

Notitiae 85, vol. 9, nos. 7–8 (July–August 1973): 247.

Reflections on Chapter IV of the *Ordo initiationis christianae adultorum*

The Sacred Congregation for Divine Worship has received a request for an interpretation of Chapter IV of the Order of Christian

Initiation of Adults, "Preparing Adults for Confirmation and the Eucharist, Who Were Baptized as Infants and Did not Receive Catechesis," in which are given pastoral suggestions for catechesis to be handed on to those already baptized, in the manner and according to the spirit of the catechumenate. The response given by the Congregation is provided.

1. Baptism is not repeatable.[1] By means of an indelible character, the permanent belonging to Christ and the Church cannot be nullified or completely lost, even if the baptized person does not become educated in the faith, or does not live in conformity to the demands of the faith, or explicitly renounces the faith.

2. The baptism in the faith of the Church received by an infant should later be lived out personally by the person baptized, accepting the call of Christ, professing the faith proper to him or her, deepening this faith ever more, and demonstrating it in active charity. As a help for these goals there should be catechesis,[2] which additionally has the task of introducing the person into the concrete life of the community, engaging the faithful person in its apostolic activity and liturgical life. Such a postbaptismal catechesis, though, is never a catechumenate. The term "catechumenate," therefore, should be avoided in this context,[3] reserving it only for "true" catechumens. Similarly, the word "election" should be avoided because this catechesis concerns a person already chosen by God in baptism.

3. The psychological situation of uncatechized Catholics may be similar to that of catechumens. Therefore, nothing

[1] See *Denz.-Schön.* nn. 110–111; 123; 1617.

[2] See *Order of Christian Initiation of Adults*, n. 296 [401].

[3] One should recall that even *The Order of Reception into the Full Communion of the Catholic Church of Those Already Validly Baptized* says, "Equating candidates with catechumens is to be altogether avoided," n. 5 [477].

forbids having their catechesis proceed according to the same order of instruction as that of the catechumens, though always taking into account the sacraments already received.[4]

If the baptismal (or confirmation) godparent is no longer alive or does not belong to the same community, another member of this community may take on the special care of the candidate.[5]

Liturgical Rites for the Catechesis of the Baptized

Catechesis is directed to and enriches everyone; therefore it can be very useful to make it visibly illustrated and deepened by liturgical actions.[6] However, because this catechesis concerns baptized or even fully "initiated" Christians, these rites should not be conceived as later catechumenal rites. They are rather a demonstration and an explanation of how much has already been done, to better understand its significance. If someone wishes to use some of the rites contained in the *Order of Christian Initiation of Adults*, which ones may they be?

1. Rite of Acceptance into the Community

The rite "by which adults are received into the community"[7] should be clearly distinguished from the rite "for Entrance into the Catechumenate."[8] At most, some ritual element could be used: The candidate could express that he or she is ready to deepen seriously his or her faith. The person who wants to help the candidate (the godparent) could express that he or she is ready to do it. There could be kept the sign of the cross, as a remembrance of the situation with the sign of the cross

[4] See *Order of Christian Initiation of Adults*, nn. 296–298 [401–403].
[5] See *ibid.*, n. 299 [404].
[6] See *ibid.*, non. 300–303 [405–408].
[7] See *ibid.*, n. 300 [405].
[8] See *ibid.*, nn. 68–97 [42–68].

before baptism, but with a different text. The introduction into the Church should happen in a way that it does not appear as the first introduction into the community, which would be a fictitious gesture, but as a new and more knowledgeable access into the living community.

The "Rite of Election or Enrollment of Names,"[9] which signifies the beginning of the last trial period for the catechumens, does not make sense for the baptized, or at most, it would express one's inscription into a serious promise for catechesis.

2. Liturgies of the Word

The Liturgies of the Word are celebrations also appropriate for uncatechized Christians.[10] These, more than presenting salvation history, teach how to *celebrate it*, and they lead to the prayer that will have present especially those who are seeking for faith and who are preparing themselves for participation at Mass.

Uncatechized, baptized Catholics, if they participate at Mass, should not be welcomed as "catechumens" before the eucharistic liturgy. They have a right to participate at it, even if, at times, it may be appropriate to introduce them gradually to the eucharistic celebration. They already have a right to mystagogy.

3. The Rites of "Handing On"

In relationship with the determined stages of catechetical preparation of the candidates, in different liturgies of the word, the "Handing On of the Creed, of the Lord's Prayer and of the Gospels" could take place.[11]

[9] See *ibid.*, nn. 133–151 [118–137].
[10] See *ibid.*, n. 301 [406].
[11] See *ibid.*, nn. 302; 181–192 [407; 147–149, 178–184].

4. Penitential Celebrations

The scrutinies, which for the catechumens are bound with the major exorcisms, have the purpose of purifying the mind and the heart, of helping against temptations and strengthening the will to devote themselves to God and to join themselves to him.[12]

In place of the catechumenal scrutinies, some penitential celebrations could be done for the baptized,[13] in order to prepare and guide them to approach the sacrament of Penance fruitfully. The rites, in principle, could be similar to those penitential rites of the ancient Church: special prayer, and blessing with the imposition of the hand.

If it is deemed appropriate, they could also be admitted to "generic prayers of exorcism" in a deprecative form, which, however, should avoid every reference to original sin and refer only to personal guilt and to temptations. One must always remember the grace of baptism received in the past and that ever more should be lived.[14]

5. Sacrament of Penance

The early Church with St. Augustine conceived the Sacrament of Penance as a "second baptism." Therefore, once the catechetical cycle conceived on the basis of the catechumenal journey has been completed, the sacrament of Penance could take the place of baptism.[15]

[12] See *ibid.*, n. 154 [141].

[13] See *ibid.*, n. 303 [408].

[14] For the anointings with the oil of catechumens, which in the *Order of Christian Initiation of Adults*, nn. 127–132 [98–103] are foreseen in the time of the catechumenate and in connection with exorcisms, that which will be said in number 5 [477] remains in force.

[15] See *Order of Christian Initiation of Adults.*, nn. 193–226 [185–230].

Only some elements of the immediately preparatory and explanatory rites of baptism could be retained:

a) The "Recitation of the Creed"[16] before or after Penance.

b) The handing on of the lighted baptismal candle after Penance.[17]

Other elements may not be included:

a) The "ephphatha" rite:[18] The baptized should profess their faith without a special preceding rite; and he or she already completely has the right to praise God and be devoted to him in prayer.

b) The anointings:[19] In no way may the prebaptismal anointing with the oil of catechumens be adopted, nor the postbaptismal anointing with chrism. Both are strictly bound to true and proper baptism.

   Furthermore the use of the oil of catechumens is foreseen exclusively for true "catechumens," as follows from its prayer of blessing.[20]

   The anointing with chrism is one of the signs that explain the conferral of baptism; the formula speaks clearly of the baptism just conferred.[21]

c) The white garment:[22] It is put on immediately after baptism and explains the baptism just completed.

[16] See *ibid.*, nn. 193–199 [185, 193–196].

[17] See *ibid.*, n. 226 [230].

[18] See *ibid.*, nn. 200–202 [197].

[19] See *ibid.*, nn. 206–207; 218; 224 [102, 228].

[20] See *ibid.*, n. 207 in *The Order of Blessing the Oil of Catechumens and of the Sick and of Consecrating the Chrism*, n. 22.—Justly there have been abolished the other anointings with this oil, as that of new priests and of bells.

[21] See *Order of Christian Initiation of Adults*, n. 224 [228].

[22] See *ibid.*, n. 225 [229].

6. (Confirmation and) Eucharist

After the sacrament of Penance has been received, there will follow, possibly on Easter night,[23] the administration of confirmation, if it has not yet been received, and of the Eucharist.

If confirmation has already been administered, prominence will be given to the renewal of baptismal promises in a particularly solemn celebration of the Eucharist that seals the catechetical journey.[24]

Also afterwards, it is advisable that caring for Christian formation be continued, until there be a certain ability to orient oneself in the regular Christian life.[25]

Rome, 8 March 1973.

Commentary

Chapter IV of the *Order of Christian Initiation of Adults* offers some pastoral suggestions for the catechesis for adults, baptized in infancy, who afterwards did not have religious instruction and have not been admitted to confirmation and the Eucharist. To these, after applying necessary reservations, also are equivalent:

a) those who, having received only the sacraments of confirmation and the Eucharist, have subsequently abandoned religious practice and desire to return to it;

b) those who, in the practice of the Christian life, desire to deepen their faith;

c) baptized children, on occasion of the catechesis for their admission to the sacraments of confirmation and of the Eucharist.

[23] See *ibid.*, n. 304 [409].
[24] See *ibid.*, nn. 217 and 219 [223–225].
[25] See *ibid.*, n. 305 [410].

In every case, this concerns the baptized who repeat or undertake the journey of catechesis.

The *Order of Christian Initiation of Adults* has put in evidence the advantage of adaptation of catechesis to the style and method of the catechumenate. Therefore, from various places it has been asked if the rites of the *Order of Christian Initiation of Adults* may be used also in the catechetical formation of baptized adults. In particular, the request has been made by the most eminent Cardinal Ugo Poletti, the Vicar of Rome, to whom the Congregation for Divine Worship has given the "Reflections" provided above.

This concerns a new problem with the possibility of later developments that touch very diverse situations, much felt in the regions of early Christianity, where one always discovers more the urgency of a continual, incisive, adapted catechesis, so that the Christian message may be better received and deepened by the baptized. The reflection that is being developed in many countries on the theme "Evangelization and sacraments" is a confirmation of the contemporaneousness of the problem.

In this phase of research, the Congregation for Divine Worship has resolutely decided to offer only some "Reflections," or landmarks for orientation, in which, though, in addition to some suggestions, has also indicated some points that seem necessary to make firm.

Baptism Is Not Repeatable

Above all it should always be clear that a baptized person, even if negligent in Christian life and in faith, cannot be considered in the same manner as an unbaptized person. That is clearly affirmed in the *Order*:[26] "Even if adults in this situation

[26] See n. 295 [400] and *The Order of Reception into the Full Communion of the Catholic Church of Those Already Validly Baptized*, nn. 5 and 7 [477 and 480]; see Secretariat for Promoting Christian Unity, *Directory*, nn. 14–15;

have not yet heard the proclamation of the mystery of Christ, their circumstance nonetheless differs from the circumstance of catechumens because they have already been brought into the Church and become children of God by Baptism. Hence their conversion is based on Baptism already received, the strength of which they should further develop." Therefore, baptism cannot ever be repeated.

Analogously, the terms "catechumen" and "catechumenate," which in the tradition of the Church indicate the group of those who preparing themselves for baptism, should not be used indiscriminately to indicate also the baptized who, under whatever form, deepen their Christian formation. Sometimes, "catechumen" and "catechumenate" are used to indicate children undergoing catechesis for confirmation and first communion, the engaged who are preparing for matrimony, etc. That creates a certain confusion. It seems appropriate that the terms "catechumen" and "catechumenate" be used in their proper sense. That does not exclude finding other similar words, such as "Neocatechumenate," "postbaptismal catechumenate," etc.

Content and Method of the Catechumenate

In the *Order of Christian Initiation of Adults* one should distinguish the directly understood object, which is the spiritual, moral, and liturgical journey of the one yearning for baptism, and the *method*, constitutive of the gradual presentation of the Christian message, adapted to the mentality and the spiritual situation of the catechumen, punctuated by the passage of periods and successive steps, indicated by the rites of the Church, which assures by them the intervention of God in an individual's life. The method of the catechumenate intends to devote itself to the whole person, and not only to the intellect,

---

see *The Order of Baptism of Children*, General Introduction: Christian Initiation, n. 4.

making the person vibrate in unison with the sanctifying action of God, by means of biblical catecheses, which become *celebrations*, and the biblical-anthropological-Christological understanding of the signs.

This method, which is that of the first centuries of the Church, as also of pagan religions and of "initiations" of primitive societies, has been rediscovered as the more fitting way also today for a true and profound catechesis, which brings to life the mystery of Christ and of the Church and conforms one's own way of living more and more to the gospel. The publication of the *Order*, itself intended principally to the "missionary" situations for the baptism of adults, has aroused in this sense a notable influx in all countries and among those that are particularly sensitive to the necessity of a vital catechesis founded on the word of God, on the relationship with the Christian community, on the action of the Church during the entire journey of catechesis, and not only in the final phase.[27]

In the wake of the catechumenal method there may thus be organized, according to the various types of catechesis, a rite at the beginning of the catechetical journey, celebrations of the word of God, various stages or steps, blessings of the candidates, penitential celebrations, some significant "rites of handing on," perhaps some prayer of exorcism in the deprecative form, holding ever present the situation of the *baptized person*. Less appropriate though seems a rite of "election": the baptized has already been chosen by God.

In particular, the grounds of guarantee, of true renewal, and of effectiveness, are respect for one of the fundamental presuppositions of the catechumenate; namely, contact with the community and with its pastor, the interest of this community,

[27] The adaptation of the catechumenal method for children who are preparing themselves for confirmation is recommended expressly in *The Order of Confirmation*, nn. 3, 12; see Sacred Congregation for Bishops, *Directory on the Pastoral Ministry of Bishops*, 1973, n. 72.

its support, participation in apostolic activity, and mutual interchange.[28]

Baptismal Pastoral Care

Besides the adoption of the method, it is certainly useful, even necessary, that catechesis always recall baptism and its rites. It should, in fact, bring about "living one's own baptism," which is the "gateway to the sacraments," the origin and foundation of the development of life in Christ, by caring, refining, and developing it up to the perfect state. In this context, the following may be useful: the recollection of some important baptismal signs, such as the sign of the cross on the forehead, the prayers of exorcism, and the formulas for the renunciation of the devil and the profession of faith. But it should be clear that it does not concern a "repetition" of rites already received, but of recalling how much has already happened in baptism and that should always be lived.

Some signs seem less authentic, such as those per se directly bound to baptism and indicative of what happened in it, such as the handing on of the white garment, indicating the beginning of the state of "new creation" just acquired with baptism, the rite of the ephphatha for a person who already participates in prayer and, perhaps, in the Eucharist of the Christian community.

In every case, there are to be avoided the prebaptismal anointing, itself ordered to the renunciation of Satan and the profession of faith, the anointing with chrism, which indicates the priestly, prophetic and royal dignity of the newly baptized, and, obviously, the water rite. This would be contrary not only to the truth, but gravely offensive to the dignity of the sacrament. Baptism is not repeated, but it is renewed continually

[28] See *Order of Christian Initiation of Adults*, n. 19 [75]; *Order of Confirmation*, n. 12.

with the profession of faith, with the participation in the sacraments, and with a holy life. The declaration given by the Congregation for Divine Worship is very opportune to make it understood that the sacrament of reconciliation is like a second baptism.

As is seen, the Congregation's declaration concerns a first reflection on a chapter of the *Order of Christian Initiation of Adults*, which has stirred up interest and initiatives for Christian formation. With it, the Congregation for Divine Worship stimulates research, laying the foundations that favor correct development in the truth.

(G. P.)
Notitiae 85, vol. 9, nos. 7–8 (July–August 1973): 274–82.